STATISTICS

Walker Maths Essentials: Statistics 5+
1st Edition
Charlotte Walker
Victoria Walker

Cover and text design: Cheryl Smith, Macarn Design
Production controller: Siew Han Ong

Any URLs contained in this publication were checked for currency during the production process. Note, however, that the publisher cannot vouch for the ongoing currency of URLs.

Acknowledgements
Cover photo courtesy of Shutterstock

The authors wish to thank past and present colleagues who have generously shared their expertise and ideas.

For product information and technology assistance,
in Australia call **1300 790 853**;
in New Zealand call **0800 449 725**

For permission to use material from this text or product, please email **aust.permissions@cengage.com**

National Library of New Zealand Cataloguing-in-Publication Data
A catalogue record for this book is available from the National Library of New Zealand

978 01 7045183 3

Cengage Learning Australia
Level 5, 80 Dorcas Street
Southbank VIC 3006 Australia

Cengage Learning New Zealand
For learning solutions, visit **cengage.co.nz**

Printed in China by 1010 Printing International Limited.
1 2 3 4 5 6 7 27 26 25 24 23

walkermathsessentials

LEFT FOOT
LEFT HAND
RIGHT HAND
RIGHT FOOT
Twister
Twister

CONTENTS

Glossary

Make your own glossary of key terms:

Term	Definition	Picture/Example
Theoretical probability		
Experimental probability		
Sample space		
Outcome		
Census		
Sample		
Population		
Descriptive variable		
Discrete variable		
Continuous variable		
Proportion		
Axis (plural: axes)		
Frequency		

ISBN: 9780170451833

Term	Definition	Picture/Example
Mean		
Median		
Mode		
Range		
Interquartile range		
Unusual points		
Cluster		
Bias		
Expected number		

The statistical inquiry cycle

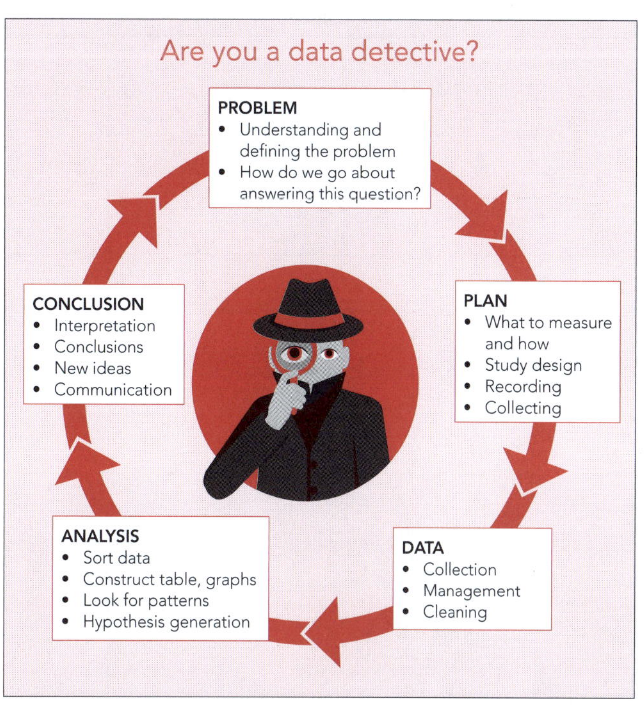

Probability

Fraction, decimal and percentage revision

Complete the table. Parts have been done for you.

Fraction	Decimal	Percentage	Probability in words
$\frac{17}{20}$			
	0.05		
$\frac{27}{80}$			
		0.6%	
		1%	Very unlikely
	0.005		
		97.5%	

ISBN: 9780170451833

Probability revision

The probability scale

- A probability value tells us **how likely** it is that an event will occur.
- We use numbers between **0** and **1** to describe probability.

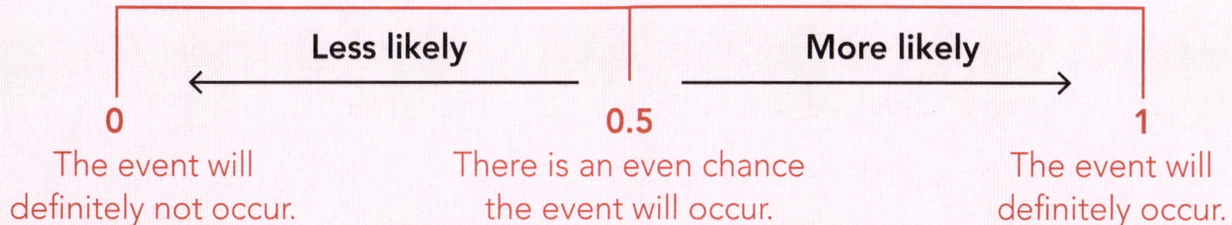

Sample space

- The **sample space** is a **list of the outcomes that can occur** when we do a probability experiment.
- You can find the sample space by drawing a **probability tree** or making a **table**.

When two events occur, draw a probability tree or make a table. E.g. Toss a coin and then pull a marble from the bag.

Draw a probability tree.

Use the tree to **list the outcomes** in the sample space:

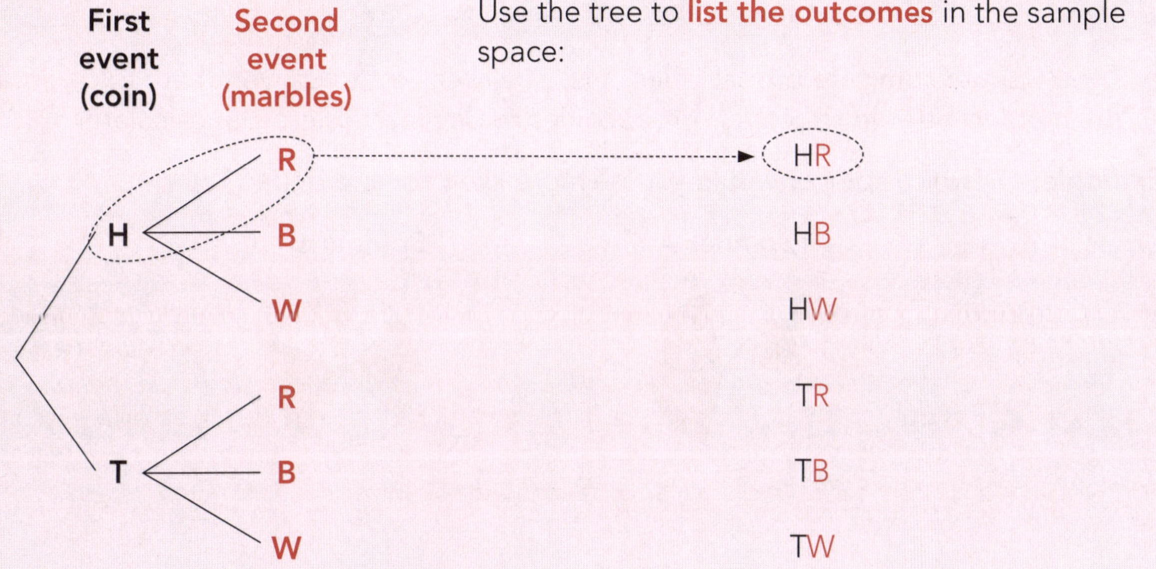

The number of outcomes in the sample space is 6.

Make a table.

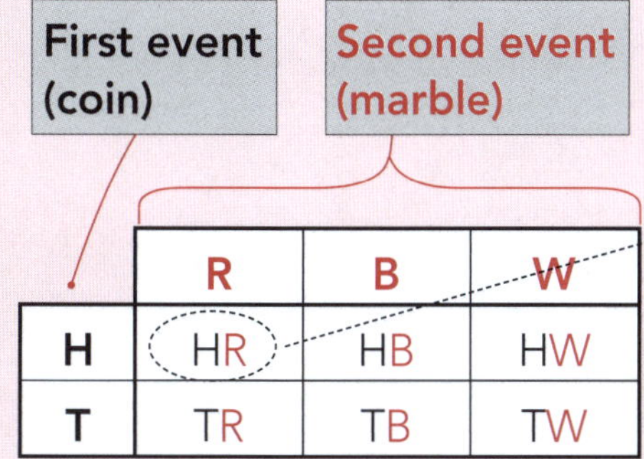

	R	B	W
H	HR	HB	HW
T	TR	TB	TW

Use the table to **list the outcomes** in the sample space:

HR
HB
HW
TR
TB
TW

The number of outcomes in the sample space is 6.

ISBN: 9780170451833

Another way of calculating the number of outcomes in the sample space:

number of outcomes for the first event (**2**) **x** number of outcomes for the second event (**3**) = **6**

Multiply

Same result.

Calculating probabilities

- Probabilities can be written as **fractions**, **decimals**, **percentages** or **proportions**.
- Sometimes, probabilities are written as '**one in** …', e.g. one in ten means $\frac{1}{10}$.
- Occasionally, reasonably even probabilities are written as a ratio out of 100, e.g. 60:40 means $\frac{60}{100}$ compared with $\frac{40}{100}$.
- When we use devices such as coins, dice and spinners, we **know** the probabilities of single events.
- We can use these probabilities of single events to calculate the probabilities of combined events.

The number of outcomes we are interested in.

$$\textbf{Probability} = \frac{\textbf{number of 'favourable' outcomes}}{\textbf{number of outcomes in the sample space}}$$

The total number of possible outcomes.

- If you want to **compare** probabilities, it is usually easiest to convert them to **decimals**.
- You need to be able to convert probabilities to decimals using your calculator.

Example: On which spinner would you be more likely to land on red?

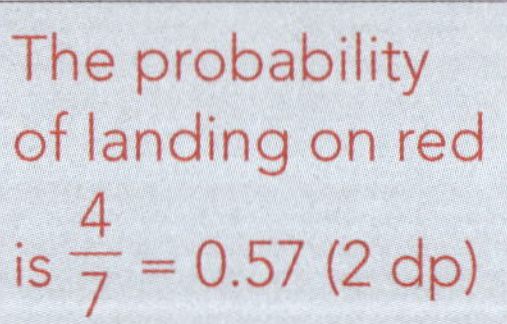

Spinner A

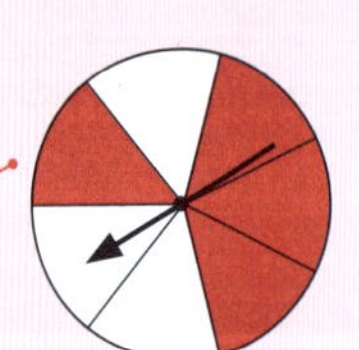

Spinner B

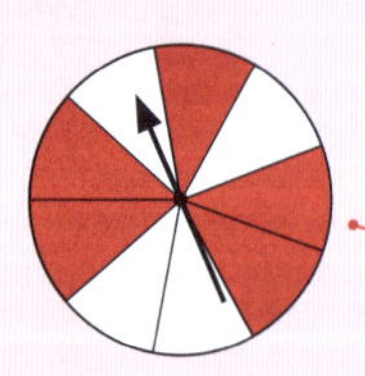

The probability of landing on red is $\frac{5}{9} = 0.5\dot{5}$

You would be slightly more likely to land on red with Spinner A.

Convert these probabilities to decimals (4 dp) and state which is more likely.

1 For spinner A, the probability of landing on red five times is 0.0609 (3 sf). The probability of tossing a coin and getting four heads is 1 in 16. Which event is slightly more likely?

2 The probability of being killed in a car crash in New Zealand in 2021 was about 0.00006. The probability of throwing a die five times and getting five heads is 1 in 7776. Which is more likely?

ISBN: 9780170451833

Expected number

- Predictions can be made based on probabilities.

Expected number of outcomes = P(event) x number of trials

Examples:

1 The probability of Anna being late to school is 0.08. There are 50 days of school next term. On how many of them would you expect her to be late?

P(late) = 0.08 x 50

= 4

2 Last year there was rain on 16% of days. How many days will we expect it to rain this year?

P(rain) = 0.16 x 365

= 58.4

We would expect it to rain on 58 or 59 days.

Rounding to a whole number is often sensible.

Answer the following questions.

1 a Rodney rolls a die 150 times. How many times should he expect it to land on a 4? ____________

b How many times would you expect it to land on a number less than 3? ____________

2 There are 20 multi-choice questions with possible answers A, B, C and D. You have no idea of the answers so pick A every time. How many answers would you expect to get correct? ____________

3 The probability of a person being right handed is 0.9. If your school roll is 1927, how many would you expect to be left handed? ____________

4 People with an extra rib make up 8% of the population. The population of New Zealand is about five million. How many people would you expect to have an extra rib? ____________

5 A clover crop can produce 70 million seeds per hectare. If one in 10 000 seeds produces a four-leafed clover plant, how many four-leafed clover seeds are produced per hectare? ____________

6 One in 200 females is colour blind. There are approximately 2.5 million females in New Zealand. How many of them would you expect to be colour blind? ____________

ISBN: 9780170451833

Ways of calculating probabilities

- There are three types of probability.

Theoretical probability — is the probability obtained from a probability model
— can be calculated where there are **equally likely outcomes**.

Note: Unless told otherwise, assume dice, coins etc. are **fair**: they produce **equally likely outcomes**.

e.g. The probability of tossing a coin and getting a head.

Some tools for theoretical probability:

Spinners

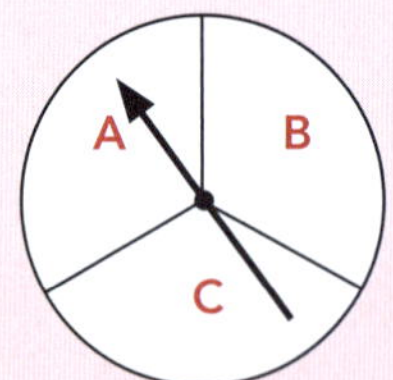

Coins

Dice or die (singular)

Bags of marbles, etc.

Experimental probability — is the probability obtained from an **experiment** or an **observational study (survey)**
— is calculated using **long run relative frequency**.

e.g. The probability of a red car passing in the next five minutes.

For both of these types:

The number of outcomes we are interested in.

$$\text{Probability} = \frac{\text{number of 'favourable' outcomes}}{\text{number of outcomes in the sample space}}$$

The total number of possible outcomes.

Actual probability — is always unknown. It is the actual probability that an event occurs.

e.g. The probability of the bus being late this morning.

Which of these can be found theoretically and which **must** be found experimentally?

1	You toss a coin and get a tail.	Theoretical	Experimental
2	Throwing a paper plane to see how far it can go.	Theoretical	Experimental
3	Surveying people at the bakery.	Theoretical	Experimental
4	Picking a pink lolly out of a mixed bag.	Theoretical	Experimental
5	Rolling a 4 on a die.	Theoretical	Experimental

ISBN: 9780170451833

Tree diagrams

- Probability trees are very useful for calculating probabilities where several events occur.
- These can be used with theoretical probability and observational/survey probabilities.

Example: There are six marbles in a bag, two red and four black. Two marbles are to be removed without looking, one at a time. The first marble **will not** be replaced.

Steps:

1 Decide what the **events** are, and their order:

Event 1 will be the colour of the first marble.

Event 2 will be the colour of the second marble.

Write the **events** at the **ends** of the branches.

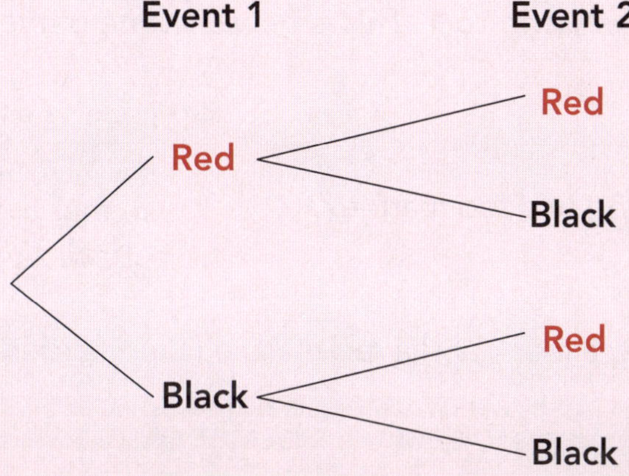

2 Add the **probabilities** of each event to the **middle** of each branch.

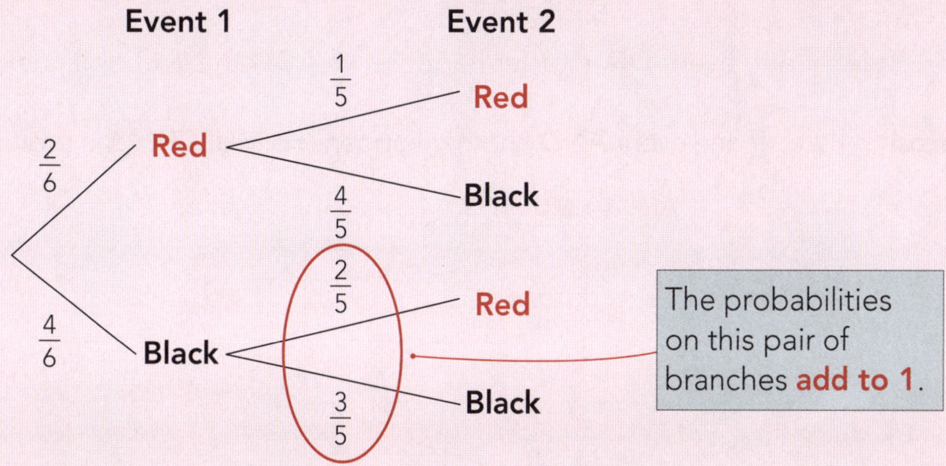

3 Check that the probabilities for every set of branches **add to 1**.

ISBN: 9780170451833

4 List the outcomes at the ends of each branch, and calculate the probability at each end. You **multiply** the probabilities along each branch because Event 1 **and** Event 2 occur.

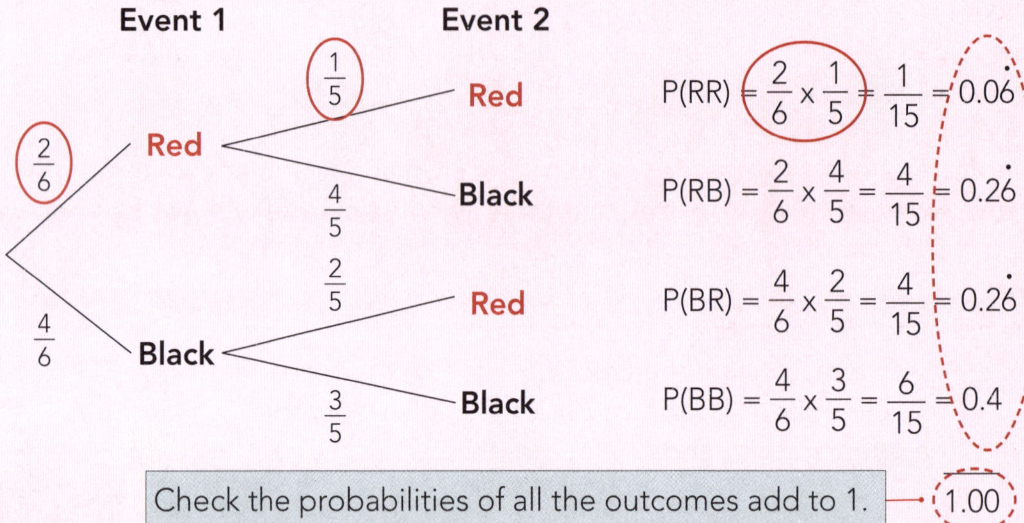

5 **Check** that your probabilities at the end **add to 1**. This is because **one** of the options **must** occur.

Note: Sometimes rounding errors mean that the sum is not exactly 1.

Now you can answer any questions.

a What is the probability of selecting two red marbles?

$P(RR) = \frac{1}{15} = 0.0\dot{6}$

b What is the probability of selecting a black and a red marble (in any order)?

$P(BR) = \frac{4}{15} = 0.2\dot{6}$ $\quad P(RB) = \frac{4}{15} = 0.2\dot{6}$

$P(BR \text{ or } RB) = \frac{4}{15} + \frac{4}{15} = 0.5\dot{3}$

c If we carried this experiment out 200 times, how many times would you expect to get two red marbles? $200 \times 0.0\dot{6} = 13.\dot{3}$ So 13 or 14 times.

Summary

1 **Addition Rule:** if one event **OR** another happens ⇒ **ADD** the probabilities.

2 **Multiplication Rule:** if one event **AND** another happens ⇒ **MULTIPLY** the probabilities.

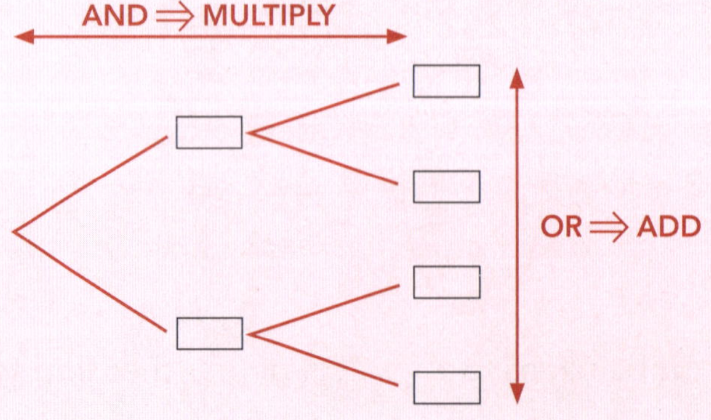

ISBN: 9780170451833

Use probability trees to answer the following questions. Give answers to 3 sf.

1 Selena had a bag containing 5 pink and 3 blue lollies. Without looking she selected a lolly then ate it. She then selected a second lolly.

a Complete the tree diagram.

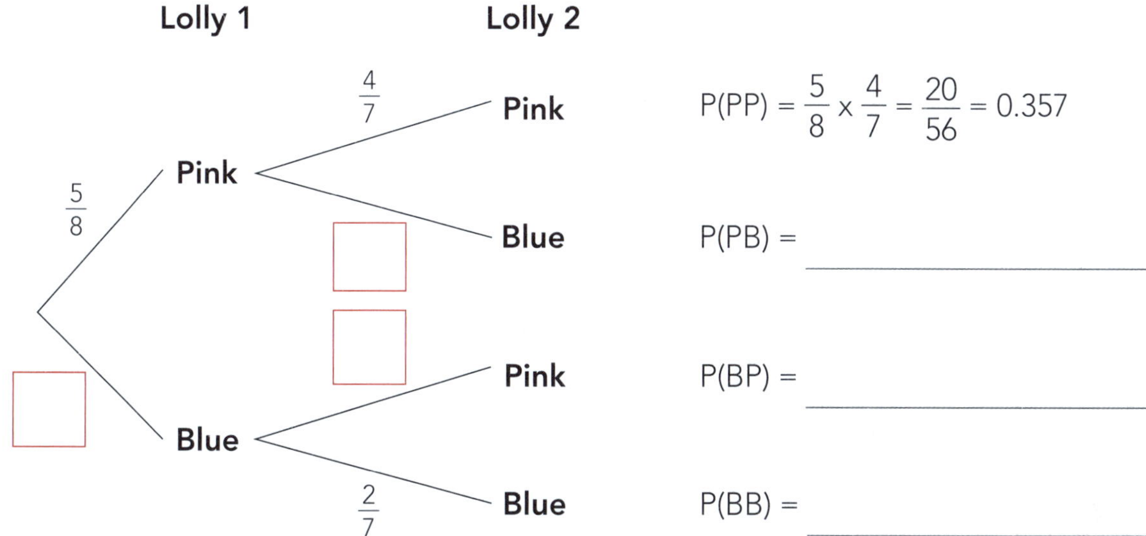

Check: Add the probabilities from the ends of each branch: ________

Add to 1? ☐

b What is the probability that she selected two blue lollies?

____

c What is the probability that she selected one of each colour?

____

d What is the probability that she selected two lollies, neither of which were blue?

____

e What is the probability that she selected at least one pink lolly?

____

f If she repeated this experiment 50 times, how many times would she expect to get two pink lollies?

____

ISBN: 9780170451833

2 Jules kicks penalties for her rugby team. There is a 30% chance it's windy on game day. When it's windy she misses the penalty 55% of the time. When it isn't windy she gets it 73% of the time.

a Complete the tree diagram.

Change the percentages to decimals.

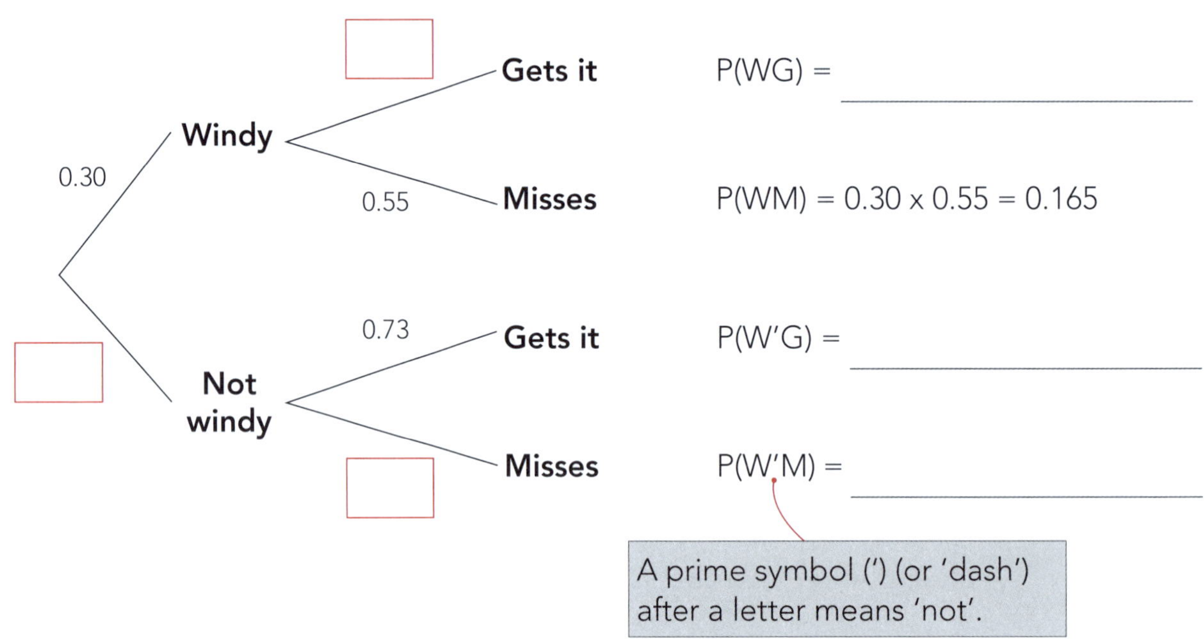

A prime symbol (') (or 'dash') after a letter means 'not'.

Check: Add the probabilities from the ends of each branch: ______

Add to 1? ☐

b What is the probability that it's windy and she gets the penalty?

______

c What is the probability that she misses the penalty?

______

d What is the probability that it's windy or she gets the penalty?

______

e What is the probability that it's not windy or she misses it?

______

f If she kicked 10 penalties on a windy day, how many would you expect her to miss?

______

  ISBN: 9780170451833

3 Katrina tosses a coin and then rolls a die.

a Complete the tree diagram.

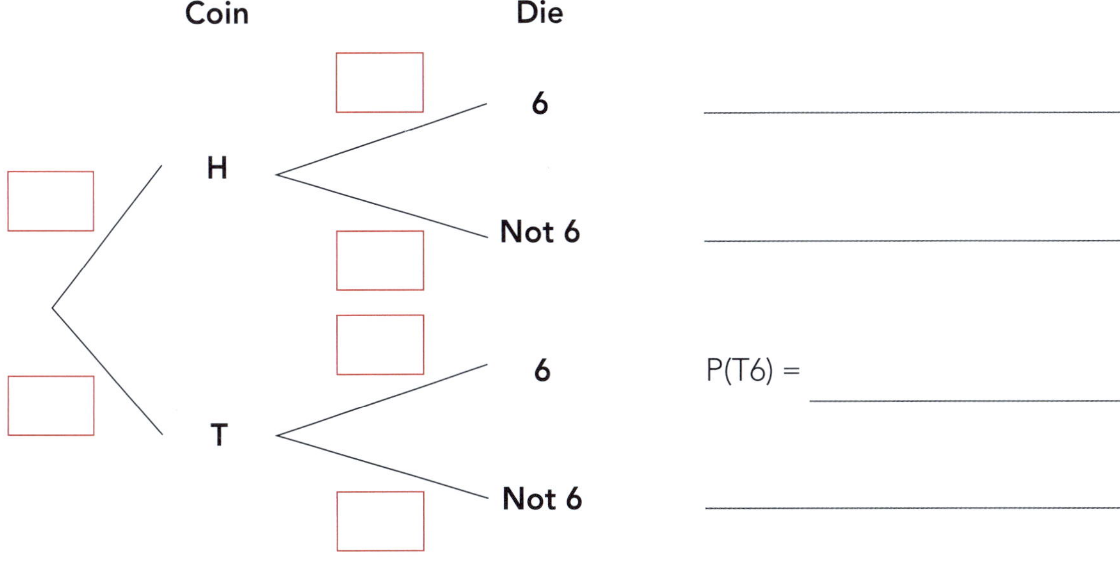

Check: Add the probabilities from the ends of each branch: ________

Add to 1?

b What is the probability that she gets tails and a 6?

c What is the probability that she gets a number other than 6?

d What is the probability that she gets heads or a 6?

e What is the probability that she doesn't get tails?

f If she repeats this experiment 50 times, how many times would you expect her to get a 6?

g If she repeated this experiment 50 times, how many times would you expect her to get heads and a 6?

ISBN: 9780170451833

4 Theodore and his four friends are planning their evening. Two of them want Hawaiian pizza while the rest want pepperoni. One of his friends wants to go to the park, the rest want to see a movie.

Complete the tree diagram.

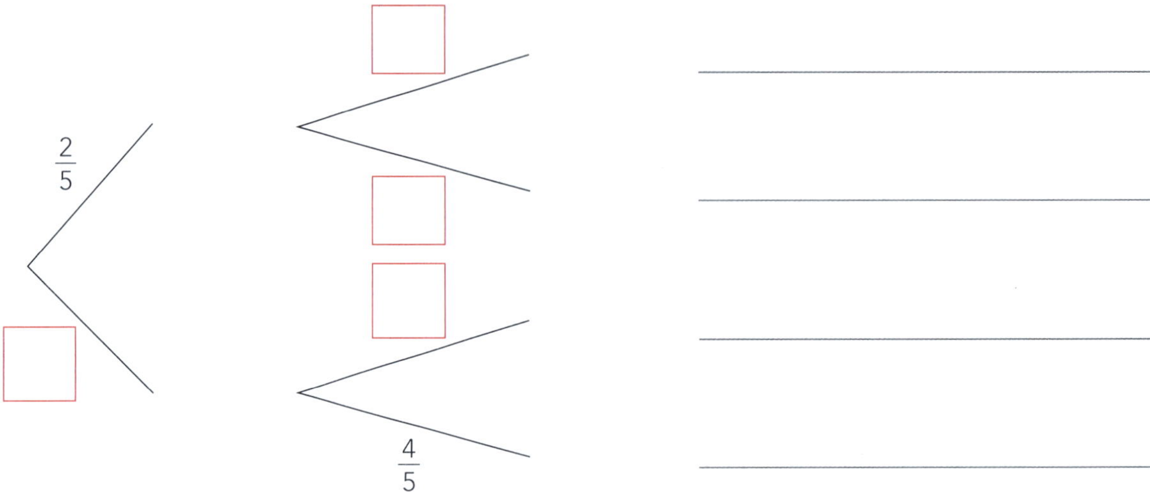

Check: Add the probabilities from the ends of each branch: ____________

Add to 1? ☐

5 Eunice and Filipe have been challenged to go skydiving. There is a 58% chance Eunice will jump. If Eunice jumps, Filipe is 67% likely to jump as well. If Eunice chickens out, the likelihood of Filipe jumping is only 14%.

a Create a tree diagram for their situation.

b What is the probability that they will both jump? ____________

c What is the probability that neither will jump? ____________

d What is the probability that just one of them will jump? ____________

 ISBN: 9780170451833

Probabilities from tables

- When there is data on two different characteristics for each member of a population, it is often convenient to display these in a two-way table.

Example: Students selected a language to learn, either Spanish or Samoan.

	Spanish	Samoan	Totals
Year 9	49	57	**106**
Year 10	36	42	**78**
Totals	**85**	**99**	**184**

What is the probability that a student is in Year 9?

$P = \frac{106}{184} = 0.576$ (3 dp)

What is the probability that a student who takes Spanish is in Year 10?

$P = \frac{36}{85} = 0.424$ (3 dp)

What is the probability that a student takes Samoan?

$P = \frac{99}{184} = 0.538$ (3 dp)

Use the data in the following tables to answer the questions. Give decimal answers to 3 sf.

1 For a shared lunch, students and staff were asked their preferences.

	Soup	Pasta	Totals
Students	53	104	**157**
Staff	5	2	**7**
Totals	**58**	**106**	**164**

a What is the probability that a randomly selected person is a staff member? __________

b What is the probability that a person wanted to eat pasta? __________

c What is the probability that a student wanted soup? $\frac{\quad}{157} =$ ______

d What percentage of staff wanted pasta? $\frac{\quad}{7} =$ ______

ISBN: 9780170451833

2 People were surveyed about whether they had ever been skiing.

	Been skiing	**Never been skiing**	**Totals**
Australian	82	215	
New Zealander	208	64	
Totals			

a Complete the table.

b What is the probability that a randomly selected person had never been skiing? ______________

c What percentage of the whole group were Australian? ______________

d What percentage of the whole group are New Zealanders who have never skied? ______________

e What is the probability that an Australian had never been skiing? ______________

f The population of New Zealand is around 5 million. Based on this survey, how many would you expect have never been skiing? ______________

3 A group of people were surveyed and asked if they were left or right handed and whether or not they could juggle.

	Can juggle	**Can't juggle**	**Totals**
Left handed		58	**93**
Right handed	186		
Totals		**303**	

a Complete the table.

b What is the probability that a randomly selected person cannot juggle? ______________

c What percentage of the group are left handed? ______________

d What percentage of the group are right handed and can juggle? ______________

e Using this information, if the population of a city is 212 000 people, how many would you expect to be able to juggle? Round your answer to 3 sf. ______________

ISBN: 9780170451833

4 Some people can roll their tongues and others can't. The following data were collected for 248 children.

	Both parents can	One parent can	Neither parent can	Totals
Child can	79		22	**169**
Child cannot		23		
Totals		**91**	**66**	**248**

a Complete the table.

b What is the probability that a child cannot roll their tongue? __________

c What percentage of the group have parents who can both roll their tongue? __________

d What percentage of the children can roll their tongue but neither of their parents can? __________

e What is the probability that a child who can roll their tongue has only one parent who can? __________

5 In 1912, the *Titanic* sank after hitting an iceberg in the North Atlantic Ocean. Unfortunately, a number of her crew and passengers died. The exact number that died is unknown. However, this table shows estimates of deaths for the numbers of first class, second class and third class passengers, and the crew.
Of the passengers, the survival rates were slightly over 25% for those in third class, but slightly under 63% for first class.

	First class	Second class	Third class	Crew	Totals
Survived		118			**711**
Died				673	**1490**
Totals	**325**	**285**	**706**	**885**	**2201**

a Complete the table.

b What percentage of second class passengers died? __________

c What's the probability a randomly selected passenger was in second class? __________

d What percentage of passengers died? __________

ISBN: 9780170451833

Statistical concepts

- It's important to understand some terms and concepts that are important in Statistics.

Census and sample

A census compared with a sample

Census
- You collect data from **every member of the population**.
- You get very accurate information.
- However, it is often impossible and usually very expensive to do.
- It is best to do a census if the answer to the question **really matters**.
- In New Zealand, a census of the population takes place every five years.

Sample
- You collect data from **just some of the population**.
- You don't get such accurate information.
- However, it is much easier and cheaper to take a sample.

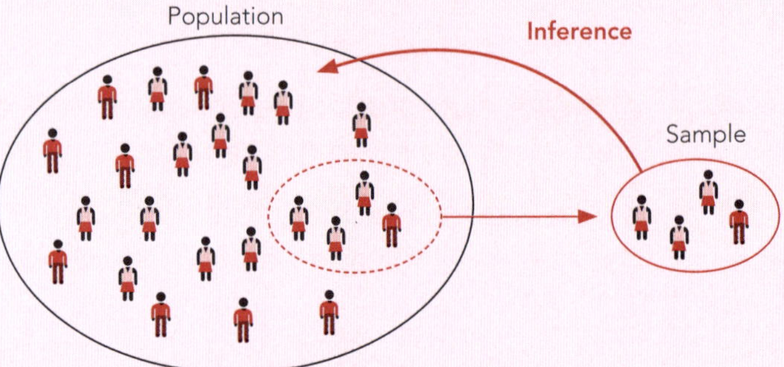

The results from the sample provide an **estimate** or **approximation** about the population. This is known as an **inference**.

Which would be more appropriate for getting information for the following situations, and why?

	Question	Census or sample?	Why?
1	Do New Zealanders want a new flag?		
2	What do New Zealanders think about a new toothpaste flavour?		
3	What is the most popular ice cream brand in New Zealand?		

ISBN: 9780170451833

Types of variables

There are three type of variables:

Descriptive variables These are **descriptions** or **names**.
Data recorded about each person/thing: **words**.
Typical question starts with 'What …'
Examples: hair colour, brand of cellphone.

Discrete variables These are **numbers** which are the result of **counting**.
Data recorded about each person/thing: **whole numbers**.
Typical question starts with 'How many …'
Examples: number of siblings, number of pants you own.

Continuous variables These **numbers** are the result of **measuring**.
They can be **fractions** or **decimals**.
Typical question starts with 'How long, heavy, etc. …'
Examples: height, weight, distance, time.

Write down which types of variables these are.

1 Favourite song ______________

2 Number of sisters ______________

3 Distance to the supermarket ______________

4 Shoe colour ______________

5 Time it takes you to eat breakfast in the morning ______________

6 Number of people who live in your house ______________

Here is some data that has been collected:

Question		Rangi	Tina	Koa
A	How long are your shoelaces?	0 cm	69 cm	120 cm
B	How many pets do you have?	3	1	5
C	How heavy was your school bag today?	3.2 kg	5.8 kg	4.5 kg
D	What is your favourite biscuit?	Belgium	Chocolate chip	Anzac
E	What colour are your eyes?	Hazel	Green	Brown

7 Which questions have answers that are descriptive variables? ______________

8 Which questions have answers that are discrete numeric variables? ______________

9 Which questions have answers that are continuous variables? ______________

ISBN: 9780170451833

Investigative questions

- There are **three** types of investigative questions.

Summary questions: investigate **one variable** at a time. This could be a word or a number.

Examples: What is your favourite fruit? — **One variable** — fruit.

How many pairs of undies do you have? — **One variable** — pairs of undies.

Comparative questions: investigate **one variable** for **two groups**.

Example: Did the boys get higher grades than girls in the science test?

One variable — science grade. **Two groups** — girls and boys.

Relationship questions: compare **two variables** for **one group**.

Example: Is there a relationship between height and arm span in Year 10 students?

Two variables — height and arm span. **One group** — Year 10 students.

Write down the type of question these are.

	Question	Type of question
1	Does ice cream melt faster than frozen yoghurt?	
2	How many pairs of shoes do you own?	
3	Are smaller laptops more expensive than larger laptops?	
4	Is there are relationship between carrot length and weight?	
5	Do Year 10 students have more money in their bank account than Year 13 students?	
6	What is the distance between your house and school?	
7	Does the length of leaves increase as they become wider?	
8	Do those who can roll their tongue talk faster than those who can't roll their tongue?	
9	Does people's sensitivity to taste decrease with age?	

  ISBN: 9780170451833

Types of survey questions

- Statistics can be gathered by observation or by questioning.
- There are a number of types of survey questions that can be asked.
- It's important to choose the appropriate type for the data that you want to collect.

Type		Description	Example
Closed	Binary	Have only two answers, often yes or no.	Did you bike to school today? Yes ☐ No ☐
	Multi-choice	More than two possible answers but defined.	What colour hair do you have? Brown ☐ Blond(e) ☐ Black ☐ Other ☐
Open	Short	Requires a one- or two-word response.	What is your favourite movie?
	Long	Allows a sentence or paragraph answer	What are your thoughts on compulsory Te Reo in schools?

Closed questions are easier to analyse statistically, but it's important to make sure they will give you the information needed to answer an investigative question.

Open questions can lead to a wide range of responses, so they are much more difficult to analyse statistically. There needs to be a good reason for using them.

What types of question are these?

	Question	Type of survey question
1	Have you had a shower today?	
2	What would you prefer for dinner? Burger ☐ Roast ☐ Salad ☐	
3	What is your happiest memory?	
4	What is your favourite food?	
5	How do you feel about the school uniform?	

ISBN: 9780170451833

Data display

- There are different ways of displaying data. Which is most appropriate depends on the **type** of variable:

Descriptive data	Discrete data	Continuous data
Tally chart Pictograph Dot plot Bar graph Strip graph Pie graph	Tally chart Pictograph Dot plot Bar graph Strip graph Line graph/time series Scatter plot Box plot	Histogram Line graph/time series Scatter plot Box plot **If rounded** Dot plot

Write the names of each graph, and the types of data for which each is appropriate.

1

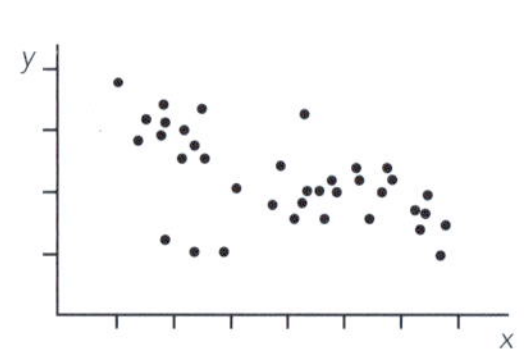

2

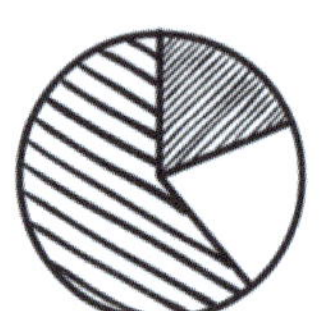

Pie graph

3

French	||||
German	𝍸 ||||
Latin	||
Spanish	𝍸

4

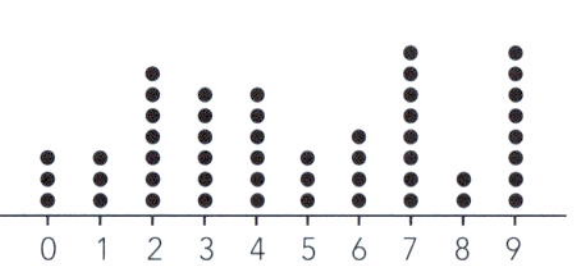

5

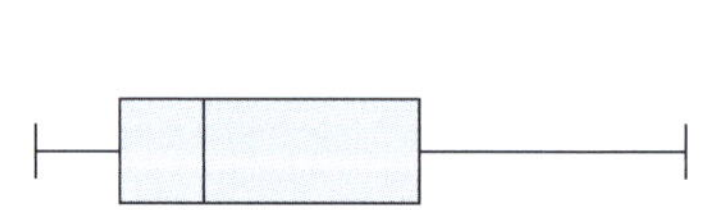

6

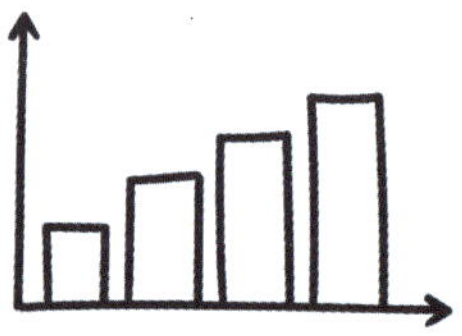

7

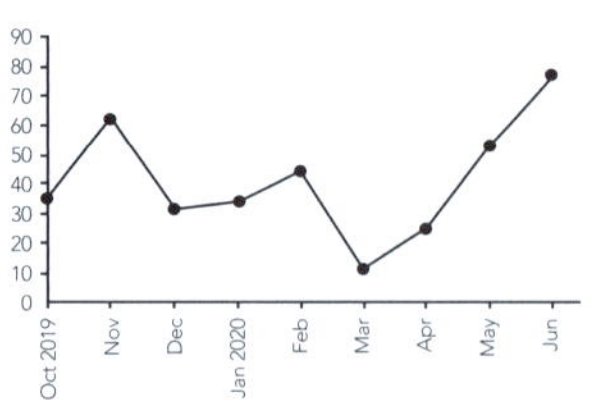

8

9

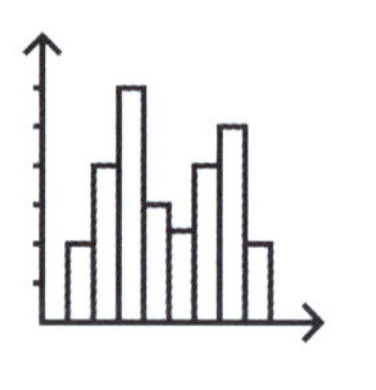

All sorts of other graphs are used, but remember, fancy doesn't necessarily mean better or easier to understand.

 ISBN: 9780170451833

Data interpretation

- When interpreting graphs, you need to explain your reasoning.
- Sometimes there are several correct answers. This can lead to interesting discussion.
- Sometimes published graphs are misleading or incorrect.
- This may be intentional or careless. It pays to **think carefully** about the information and who presented it.

Example:

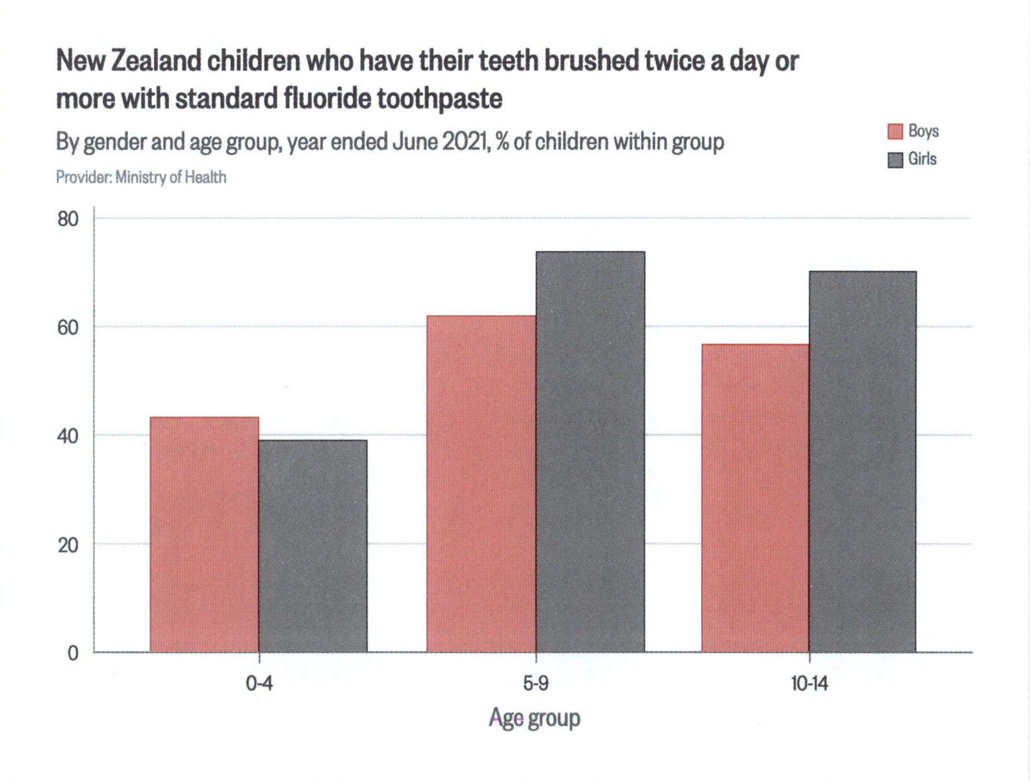

Girls are better at brushing their teeth than boys.

☑ Agree ☐ Disagree ☐ Can't tell for sure

Explain your answer. There is a higher percentage of girls who are brushing their teeth between the ages of 5 and 14.

You can agree or disagree or say you can't tell for sure with the statement. It is your reasoning that makes you correct or incorrect.

☐ Agree ☐ Disagree ☑ Can't tell for sure

Explain your answer. More girls are brushing their teeth aged 5–14, but this doesn't mean they are doing a better job than the boys.

ISBN: 9780170451833

Pie graphs

- Pie graphs are appropriate for **descriptive** data.
- They are best used when there are relatively few divisions of the data.
- The area of each sector is proportional to the frequency of each variable.
- **Single** pie graphs are used to plot the data obtained from answers to a **summative question**.

Understanding pie graphs

Example: This data is from Surf NZ and analyses the equipment used for rescues. IRB stands for Inflatable Rescue Boat and RWC stands for Rescue Water Craft or jet ski.

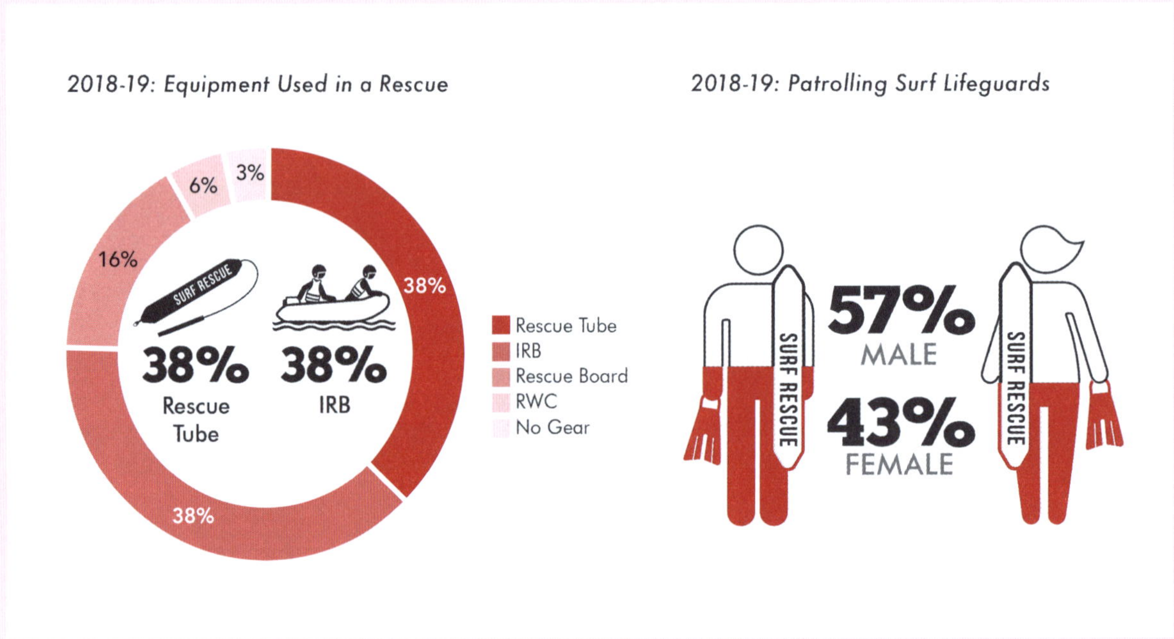

1 Suggest a question that could be used to collect the data in the pie graph.

What equipment was used in each rescue during 2018 and 2019?

2 What sort of question is this? Summative

3 What percentage of rescues used some sort of equipment? 100 – 3 = 97%

4 What percentage of rescues used a rescue board? 16%

5 What is the probability that you are rescued by a female lifeguard with a rescue tube?

P = 0.43 x 0.38 = 0.1634

ISBN: 9780170451833

Answer the following questions. Give your answers to 3 sf.

1 When someone has an accident they are often supported by the Accident Compensation Corporation (ACC). This pie graph shows new claims to ACC in 2021.

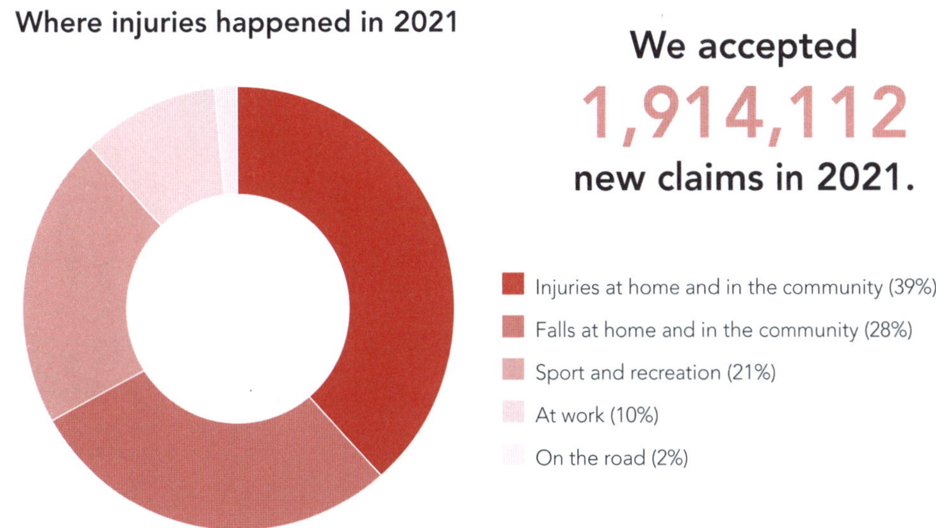

a Suggest a question that could be asked in order to obtain this data.

____

b What type of question is this? _______________

c What proportion of new claims resulted from incidents either on the road or at work? _______________

d How many claims occurred as a result of sport and recreation? Round your answer to 3 sf. _______________

e Which category was responsible for about 190 000 claims? _______________

f Calculate the probability that a claim resulting from an incident at home or in the community was a fall. _______________

g Most new claims resulted from incidents at home or in the community.

☐ Agree ☐ Disagree ☐ Can't tell for sure

Explain your answer.

____

____

ISBN: 9780170451833

2 NZ Post annually reviews eCommerce in New Zealand. These pie graphs display the ages and genders of online adult shoppers in 2020. Assume that the gender distribution is the same across all age groups.

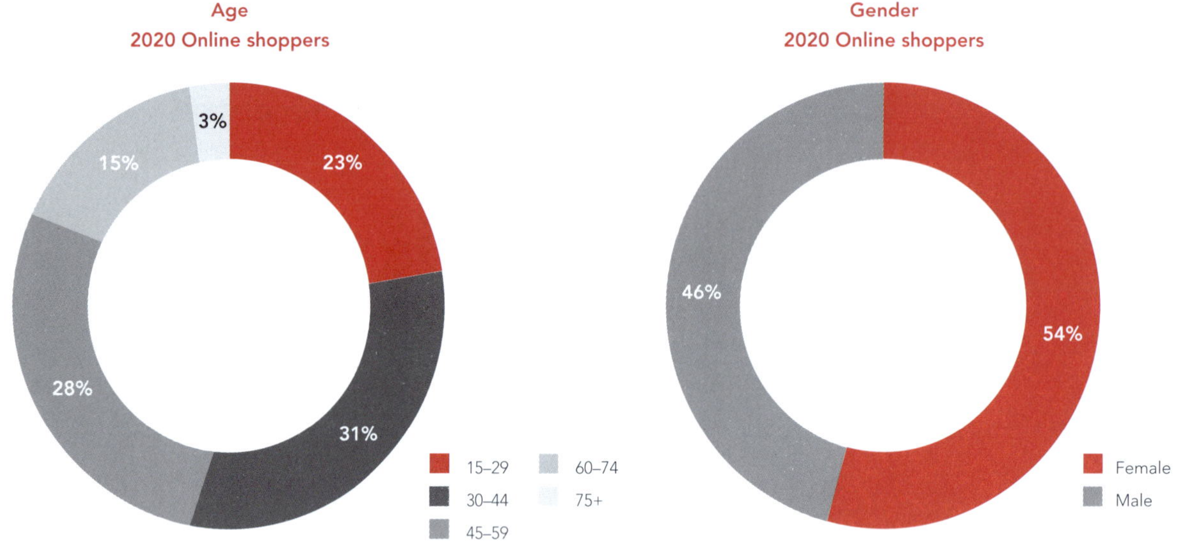

2.13M
ADULT KIWIS SHOPPED ONLINE IN 2020

52%
OF KIWIS SHOPPED ONLINE IN 2020

306K
KIWIS SHOPPED ONLINE FOR THE FIRST TIME IN 2020

a What percentage of online shoppers were between 60 and 74 years old? __________

b What percentage of online shoppers were under 45 years old? __________

c What percentage of online shoppers were female and between 15 and 29 years old? __________

d Name another suitable graph for the age data. __________

e Estimate the number of adult females that shopped online in 2020. __________

f Calculate the probability that an adult New Zealander was over 75 years old and shopped online. __________

ISBN: 9780170451833

3 These graphs show the values of global cat and dog food markets.

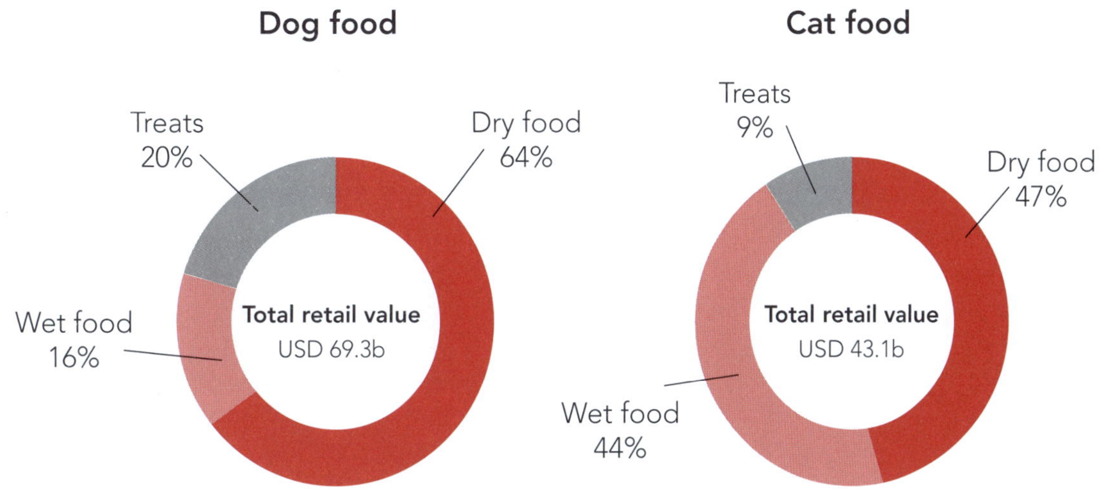

a What is the value of the global market for dry dog food? ______

b What is the total value of the market for wet pet food? ______

c What proportion of the total value of pet foods is dry dog food? ______

d Excluding treats, 20% of the dog food market is wet food. True/False

Justify your answer: ______

______

e The dog treat market is worth just over double the cat treat market. True/False

Justify your answer: ______

______

f New Zealand produced NZ$261 million worth of pet food in 2021. Assume that this value remains the same in 2022, and NZ$1 = US$0.64. What percentage of the global pet food market does New Zealand have?

______

______

ISBN: 9780170451833

Bar graphs

- Bar graphs are used to display **discrete** or **descriptive** data.
- They are sometimes known as column graphs.
- They can be plotted **vertically** or **horizontally**.
- The bars always have **gaps** between them.
- **Single** bar graphs are used to plot the data obtained from answers to a **summative question**.
- **Double** bar graphs are used to plot the data obtained from answers to a **comparative question**.

Understanding bar graphs

Example: This data is from Surf Life Saving NZ. It shows the numbers of volunteer and contract (paid) patrols.

It would have been collected in response to the **comparative question** 'What is the difference between the numbers of volunteer and contract patrols in the different regions of New Zealand?'

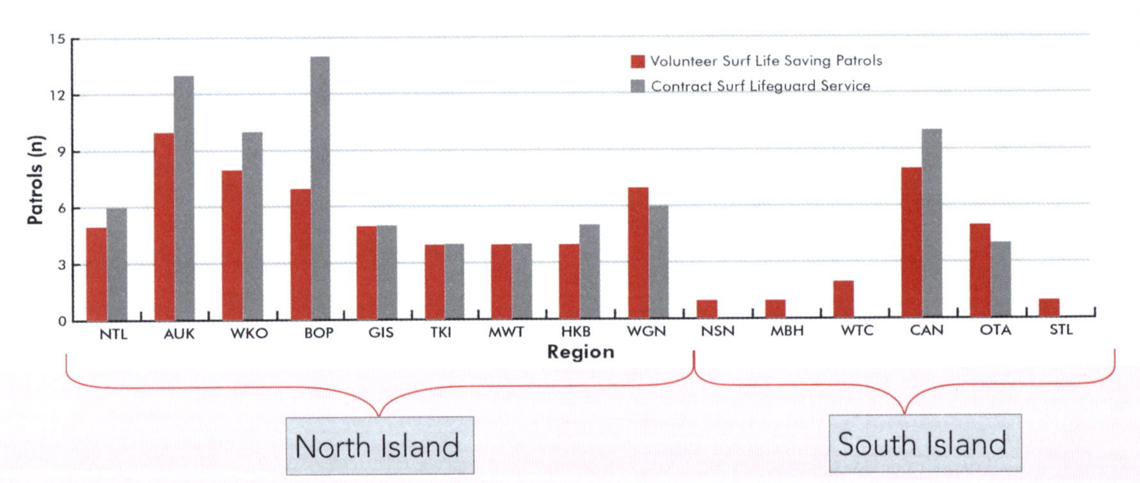

1 How many volunteer surf patrols are there in Northland (NTL)? 5

2 How many contract surf patrols are there in the South Island? 14

Only Canterbury (CAN) and Otago (OTA) have contract surf patrols.

3 One region has twice as many contract surf patrols as volunteer surf patrols.

Which region is it? Bay of Plenty (BOP)

4 If you are rescued by a surf patrol in the Waikato (WKO), what is the probability that your rescue was carried out by a volunteer patrol?

$$\frac{8}{8+10} = 0.\dot{4}$$

ISBN: 9780170451833

Answer the following questions. Give any calculations to 3 sf.

1 Read NZ conducted a reading survey of New Zealand adults in 2021.

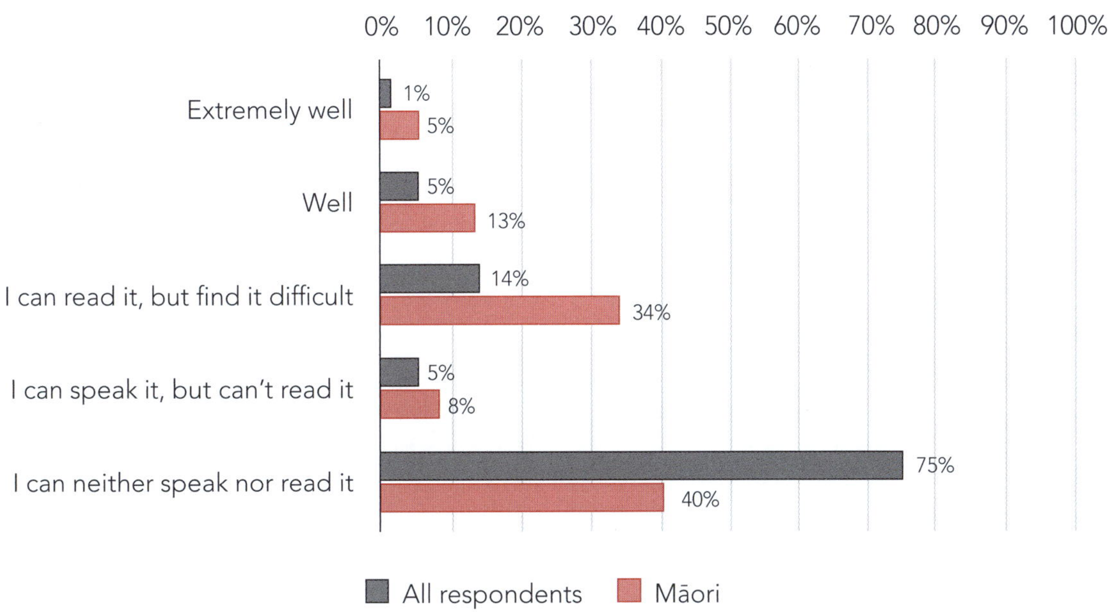

a Suggest a question that this data could be used to answer.

____

____

b What type of question is this? __________

c What percentage of Māori respondents identified that they can read Te Reo Māori well or extremely well? __________

d What proportion of all respondents could either speak or read Māori to some extent? __________

e '75% of the New Zealand population can neither speak nor read Te Reo Māori.'

☐ Agree ☐ Disagree ☐ Can't tell for sure

Explain your answer.

____

____

ISBN: 9780170451833

2 ACC collected information on new sport injury claims made by team sports players between 2019 and 2021.

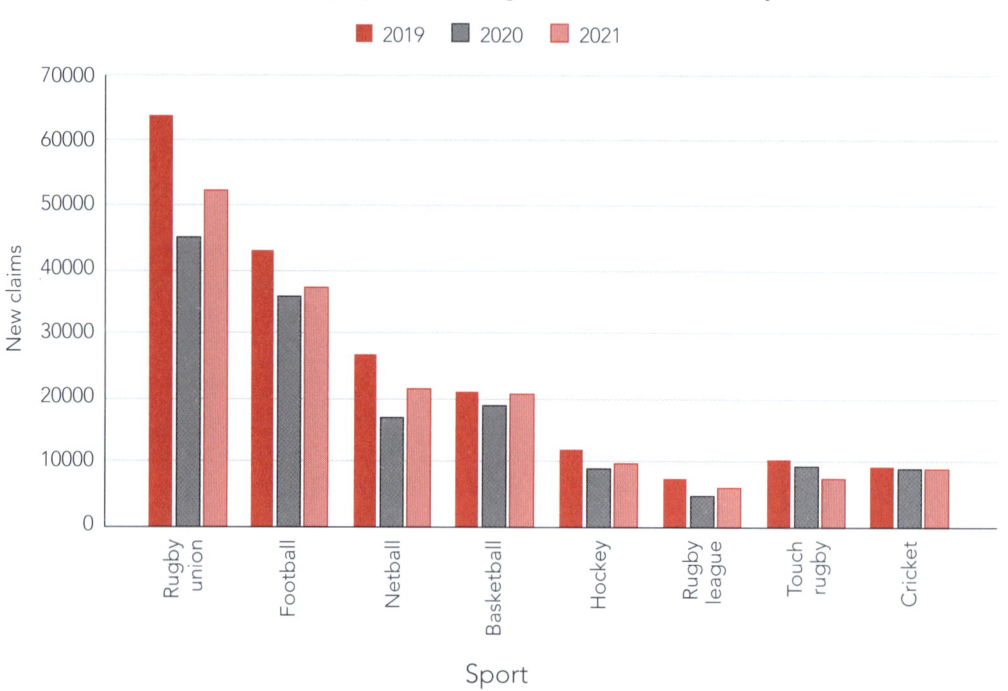

a In which year were the fewest claims made in rugby union? ______________

b Which sport had a reduction of claims in 2021? ______________

c All of the winter sports had a reduction of claims in 2020. Suggest a reason for this.

____

____

d 'Rugby union is the most dangerous team sport in New Zealand.'

☐ Agree ☐ Disagree ☐ Can't tell for sure

Explain your answer.

____

____

e 'Touch rugby is becoming safer.'

☐ Agree ☐ Disagree ☐ Can't tell for sure

Explain your answer.

____

____

 ISBN: 9780170451833

Stacked bar graphs

- Stacked bar graphs are used to display **discrete** or **descriptive** data.
- They could be considered a form of strip graph.
- They can be plotted **vertically** or **horizontally**.
- The bars always have **gaps** between them.

Understanding stacked bar graphs

Example: NZ Post annually reviews the eCommerce in New Zealand. This stacked bar graph displays the international and domestic spending on eCommerce during 2020.

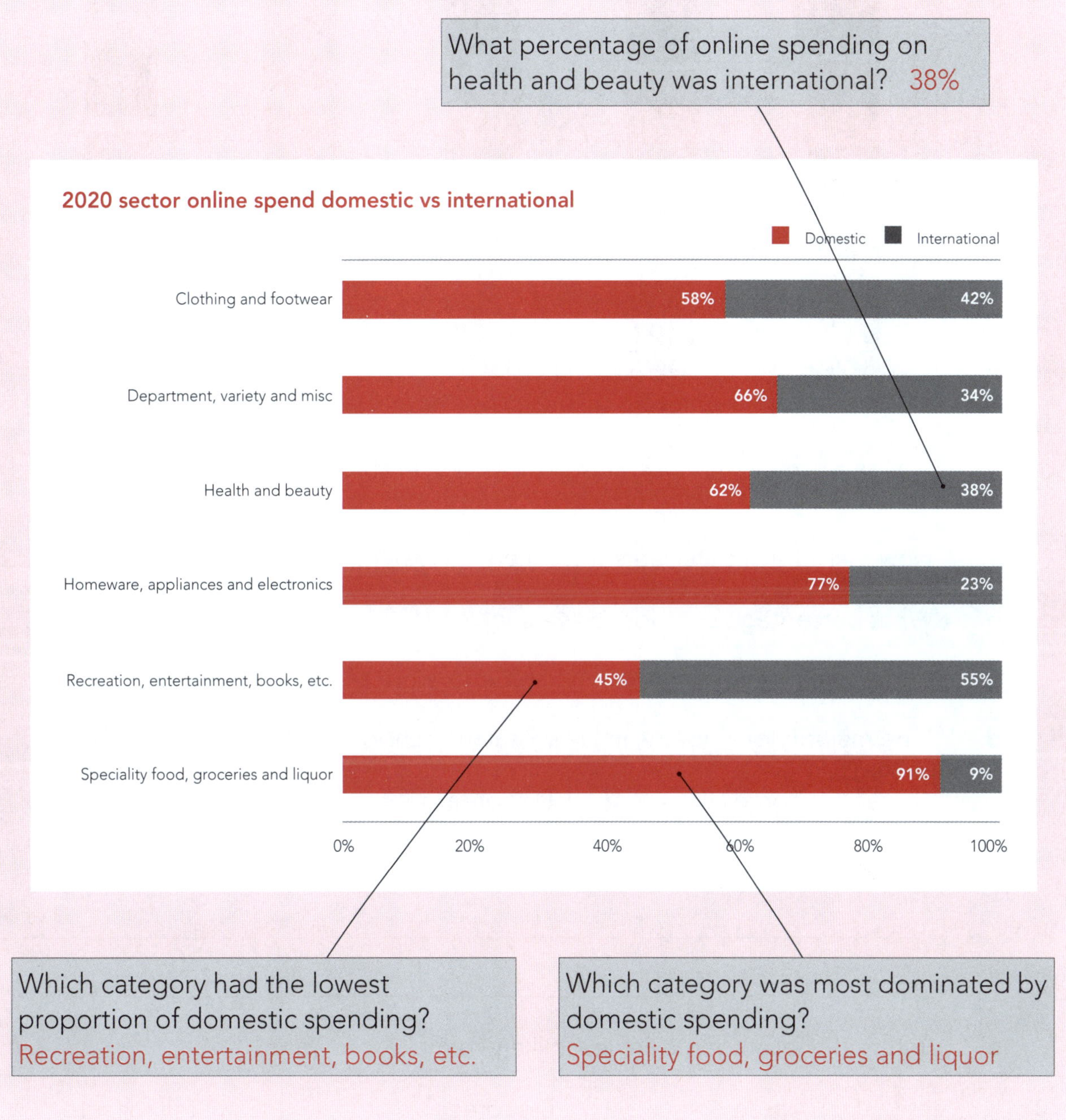

ISBN: 9780170451833

3 The Ministry of Education collects data on schools each year. In 2021, a total of 293 571 students were enrolled in schools.

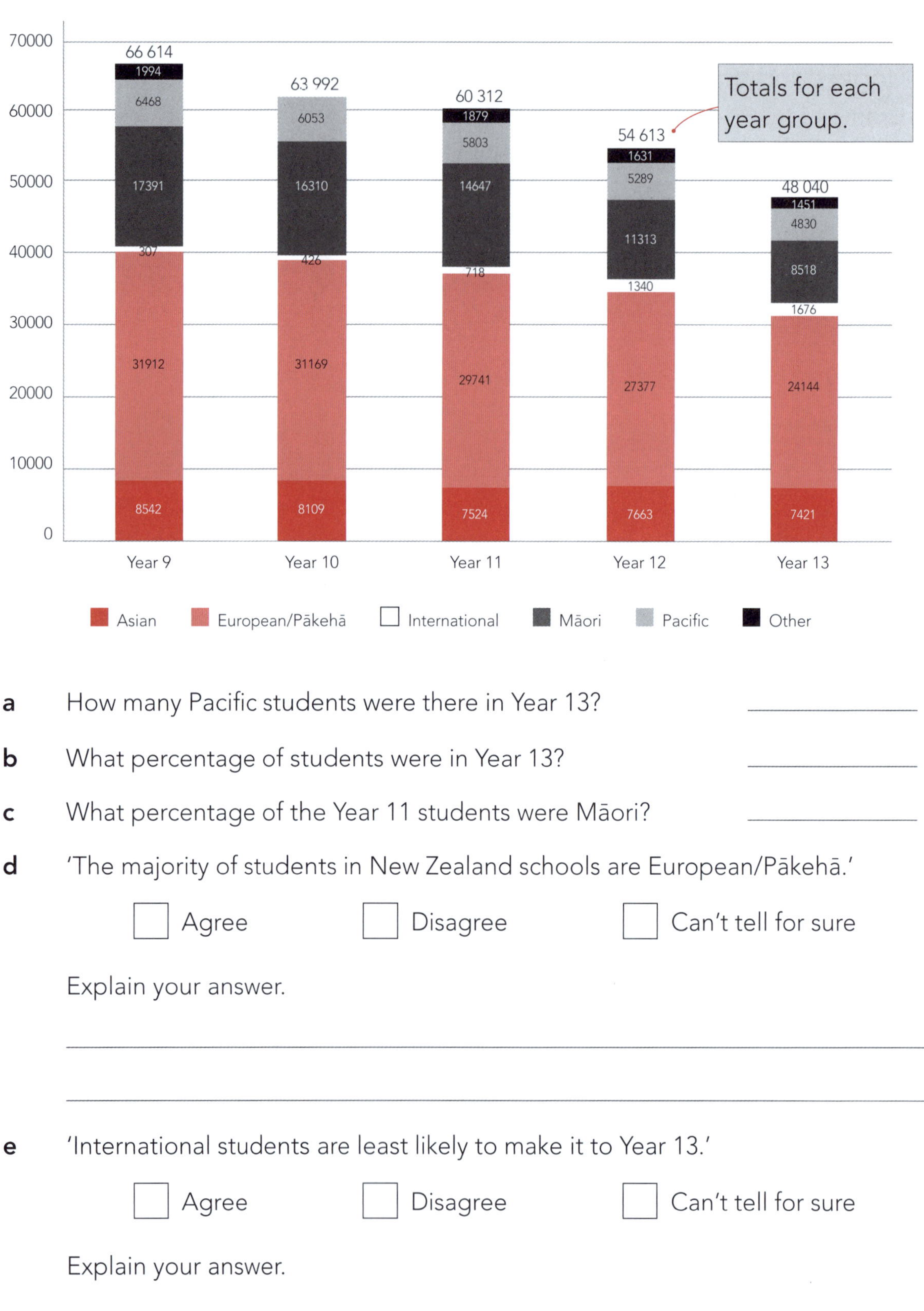

a How many Pacific students were there in Year 13? __________

b What percentage of students were in Year 13? __________

c What percentage of the Year 11 students were Māori? __________

d 'The majority of students in New Zealand schools are European/Pākehā.'

☐ Agree ☐ Disagree ☐ Can't tell for sure

Explain your answer.

____

____

e 'International students are least likely to make it to Year 13.'

☐ Agree ☐ Disagree ☐ Can't tell for sure

Explain your answer.

____

____

  ISBN: 9780170451833

Bar graphs with added extras

Example: NZ Post annually reviews eCommerce in New Zealand. This bar graph displays the growth of international and domestic eCommerce between 2019 and 2020.

Spend: total value of eCommerce.

Transactions: the number of eCommerce transactions.

Basket size: the average value of each eCommerce transaction.

The bars display the percentage **growth**, so some are negative.

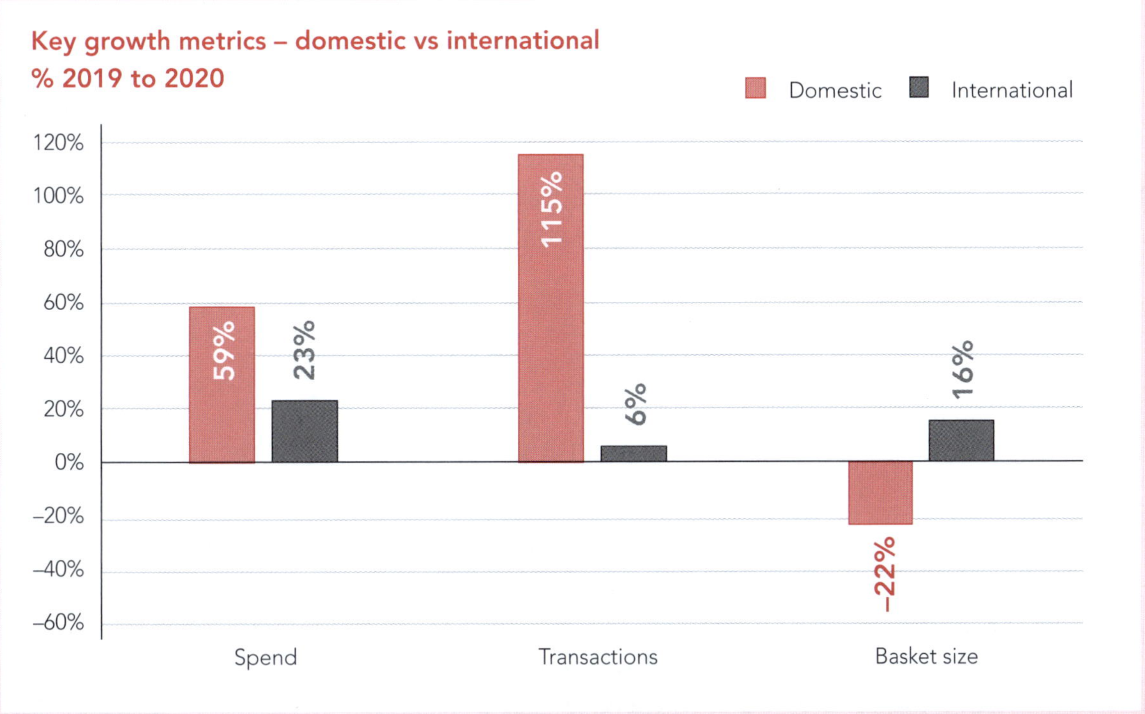

1 How much has the total number of eCommerce domestic transactions grown between 2019 and 2020?

115%. This means it has more than doubled.

2 How much has the average value of each domestic eCommerce transaction (basket size) grown between 2019 and 2020?

–22%. This means it hasn't grown, but it has shrunk by 22%.

3 Summarise the changes between 2019 and 2020 for domestic transactions.

Overall, more money was spent on a larger number of transactions, but the average value of each transaction was less.

ISBN: 9780170451833

4 The Ministry of Education collects data on schools each year.

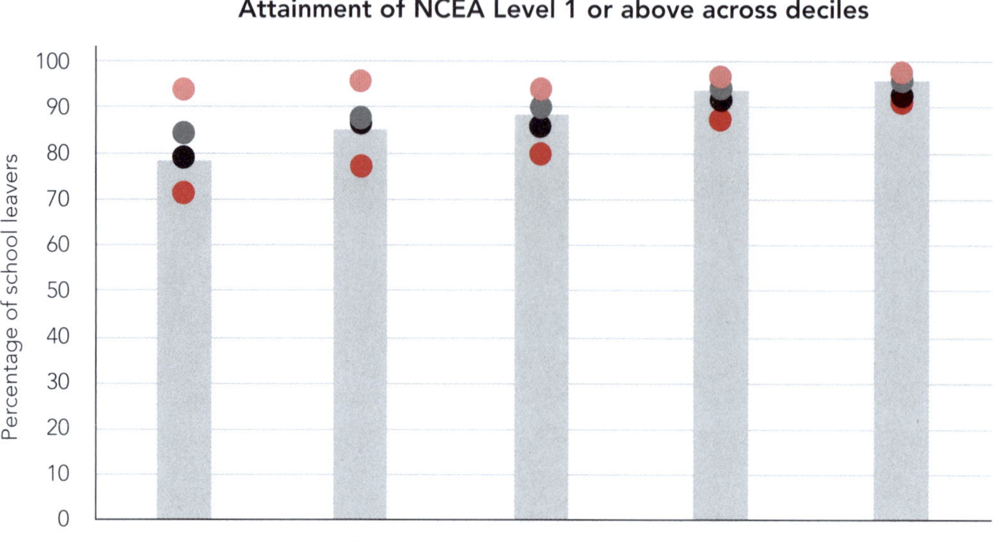

a Approximately what percentage of school leavers from Decile 3–4 schools leave with NCEA Level 1 or above? ______________

b Which ethnicity has the highest chance of leaving with NCEA Level 1? ______________

c Approximately what percentage of Pacific students from a Decile 5–6 school leave with NCEA Level 1? ______________

d 'Most students leave school with NCEA Level 1.'

☐ Agree ☐ Disagree ☐ Can't tell for sure

Explain your answer.

____

____

e 'In Decile 1–2 schools, more Pacific students leave with Level 1 than European/Pākehā students.'

☐ Agree ☐ Disagree ☐ Can't tell for sure

Explain your answer.

____

____

 ISBN: 9780170451833

5 NZ Post annually reviews the eCommerce in New Zealand. This bar graph displays the spending in different sectors between 2019 and 2020.

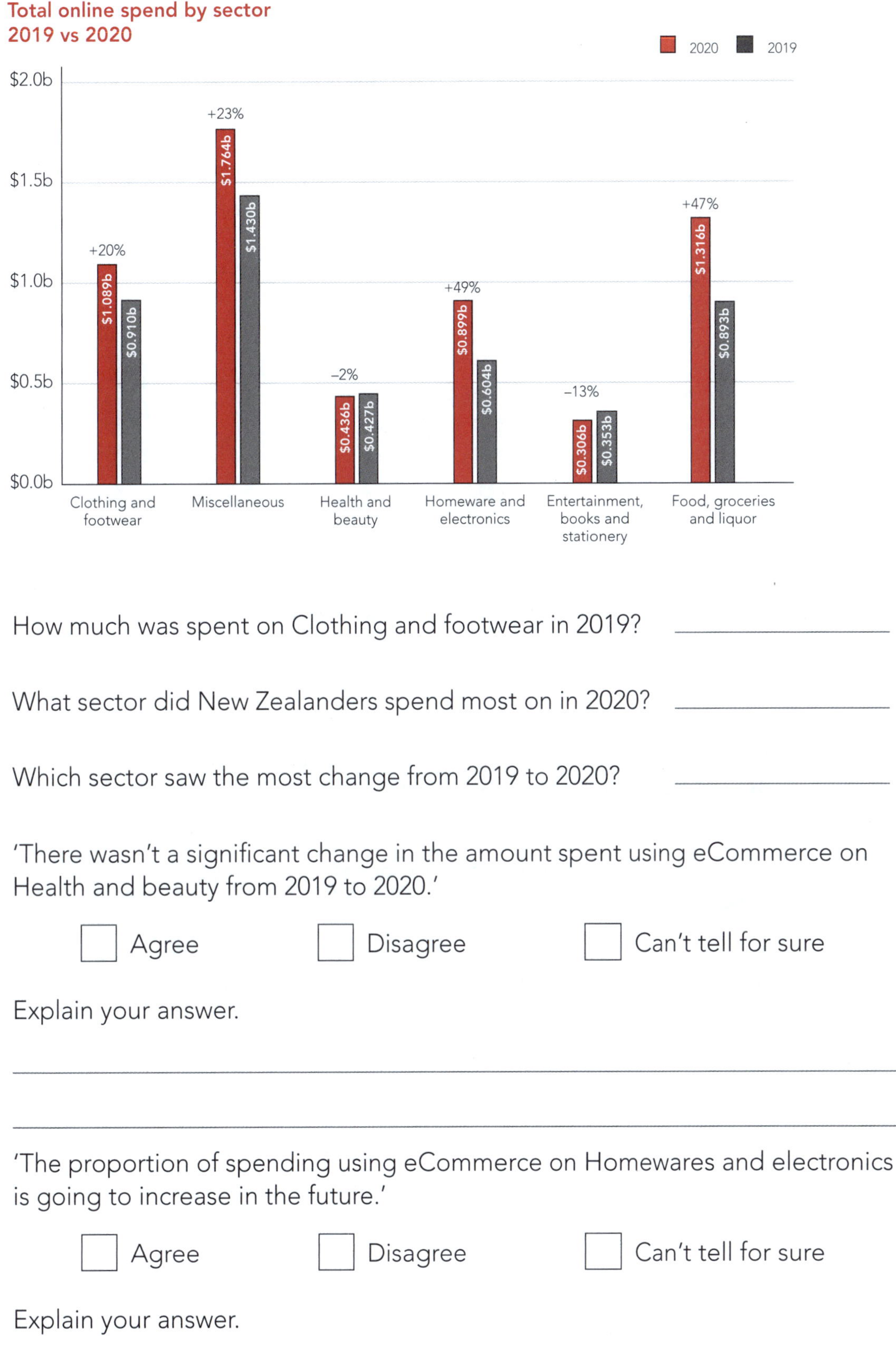

a How much was spent on Clothing and footwear in 2019? ______________

b What sector did New Zealanders spend most on in 2020? ______________

c Which sector saw the most change from 2019 to 2020? ______________

d 'There wasn't a significant change in the amount spent using eCommerce on Health and beauty from 2019 to 2020.'

☐ Agree ☐ Disagree ☐ Can't tell for sure

Explain your answer.

____

____

e 'The proportion of spending using eCommerce on Homewares and electronics is going to increase in the future.'

☐ Agree ☐ Disagree ☐ Can't tell for sure

Explain your answer.

____

____

ISBN: 9780170451833

6 NZ on Air and the Broadcasting Standards Authority analysed the use by tamariki of media in 2020.

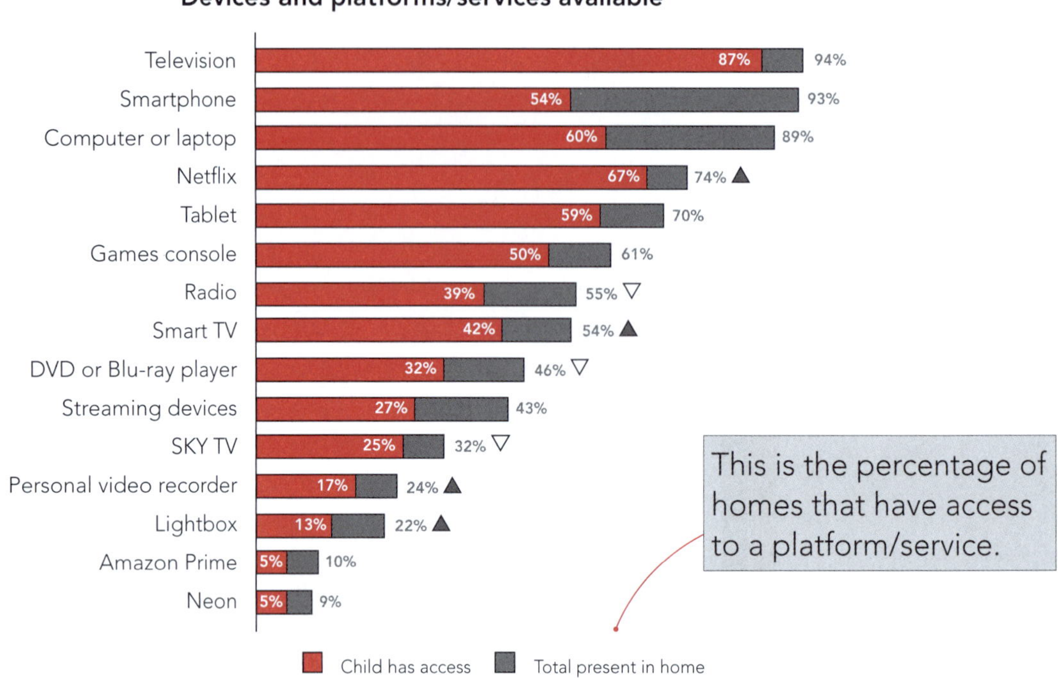

The arrows ▲ ▽ indicate a significant increase or decrease from 2014.

a What is the most common device or platform/service? ____________________

b In what percentage of homes that have access to Sky TV, do the tamariki have access to it? ____________________

c What percentage of homes have access to a games console? ____________________

d For which device or platform/service does the smallest proportion of homes allow tamariki access to it? ____________________

Explain your answer.

____

e 'If a household has a tablet, then tamariki have access to it most of time.'

☐ Agree ☐ Disagree ☐ Can't tell for sure

Explain your answer.

____

____

ISBN: 9780170451833

Challenge 1

This data is from Surf NZ.

There are two vertical axes: Left: Numbers of fatal drownings (n)
Right: Drowning rate (per 100 000 the population)

2009-19: Total Number of New Zealand Beach and Coastal Fatal Drownings per Year (n=320); Comparison of New Zealand vs Australian Beach and Coastal Fatal Drowning Rates per 100,000 pop.

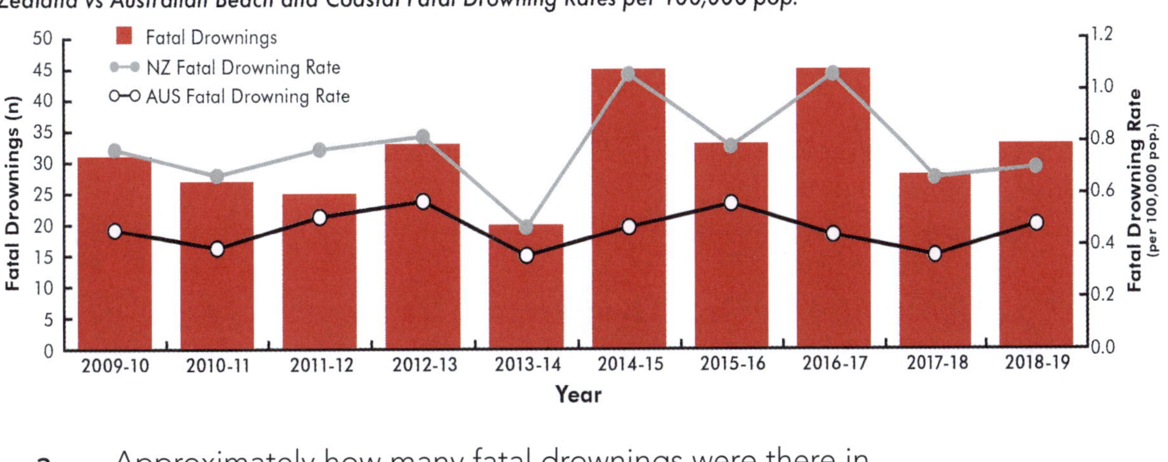

a Approximately how many fatal drownings were there in total in 2017–18? __________

b Approximately what was the Australian fatal drowning rate in 2010–11? __________

c New Zealand's fatal drowning rate peaked at around 1.1 in what years? __________

d In which year were there fewest drownings in New Zealand? __________

e 'New Zealand is a more dangerous place to swim than Australia.'

☐ Agree ☐ Disagree ☐ Can't tell for sure

Explain your answer.

____

____

f 'This graph doesn't take population into account.'

☐ Agree ☐ Disagree ☐ Can't tell for sure

Explain your answer.

____

____

ISBN: 9780170451833

Line graphs

- Line graphs are often used to show how **discrete** or **continuous** data changes at regular intervals of time.
- Lines connect the plotted points.
- When time is on the *x*-axis, these are called **time series** graphs.
- **Single** line graphs are used to plot the data obtained from answers to a **summative question**.
- **Double** line graphs are used to plot the data obtained from answers to a **comparative question**.

Quarterly data

Time series data is often given **quarterly**. This means data points are given for every quarter throughout the year.

Quarter 1 (Q1) is data from the start of January, through February and to the end of March.

Quarter 2 (Q2) is data from the start of April, through May and to the end of June.

Quarter 3 (Q3) is data from the start of July, through August and to the end of September.

Quarter 4 (Q4) is data from the start of October, through November and to the end of December.

Understanding line graphs

Example: The graph shows the average price per kilogram of kūmara, broccoli and courgettes (zucchini) in New Zealand during January of each year.

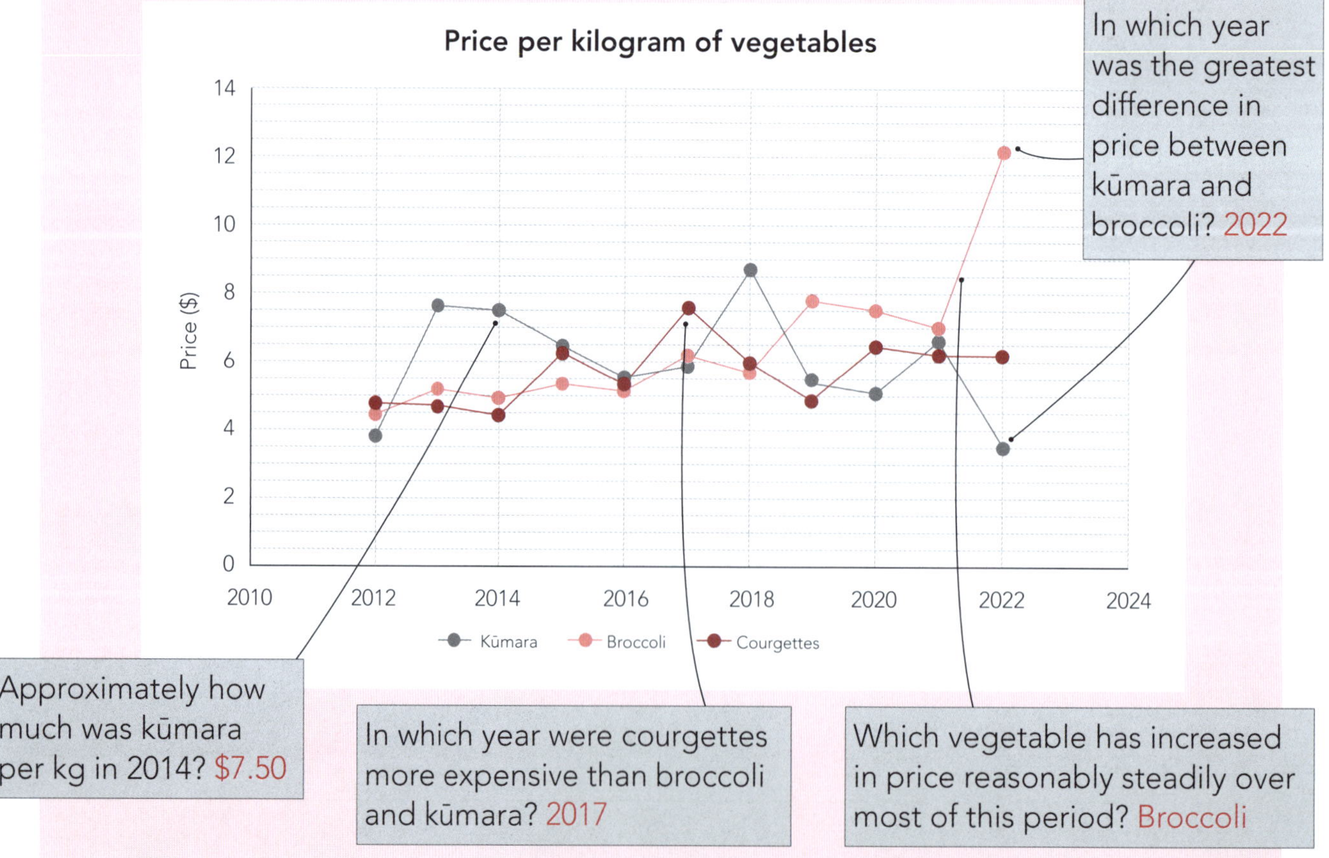

 ISBN: 9780170451833

Answer the following questions. Round any calculations to 3 sf.

1 The graph shows the unemployment rate in New Zealand adults between 2018 and 2021.

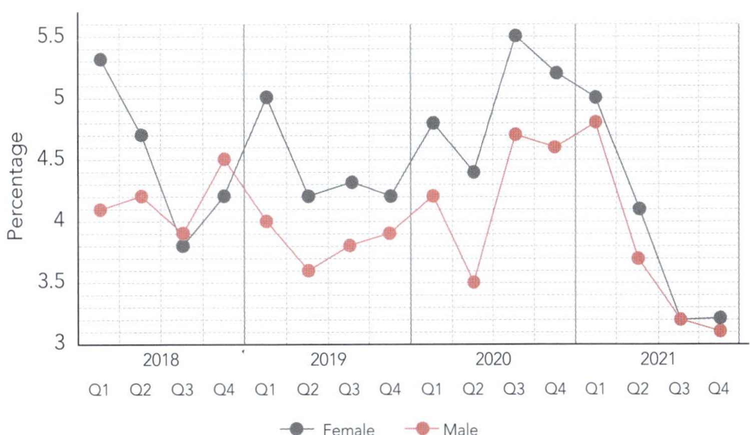

a Suggest a question that this data could be used to answer.

____

b What type of question is this? __________

c What percentage of females were unemployed in Q1 of 2020? __________

d What's the difference between male and female unemployment rates in 2018 Q4? __________

e When was the unemployment rate higher for males than females? __________

f When was the unemployment for males and females the same? __________

g 'More females are unemployed than males.'

☐ Agree ☐ Disagree ☐ Can't tell for sure

Explain your answer.

____

____

h 'Males are paid more than females.'

☐ Agree ☐ Disagree ☐ Can't tell for sure

Explain your answer.

____

____

ISBN: 9780170451833

2 NZ Post annually reviews the eCommerce in New Zealand. This line graph displays the spending during 2019 and 2020.

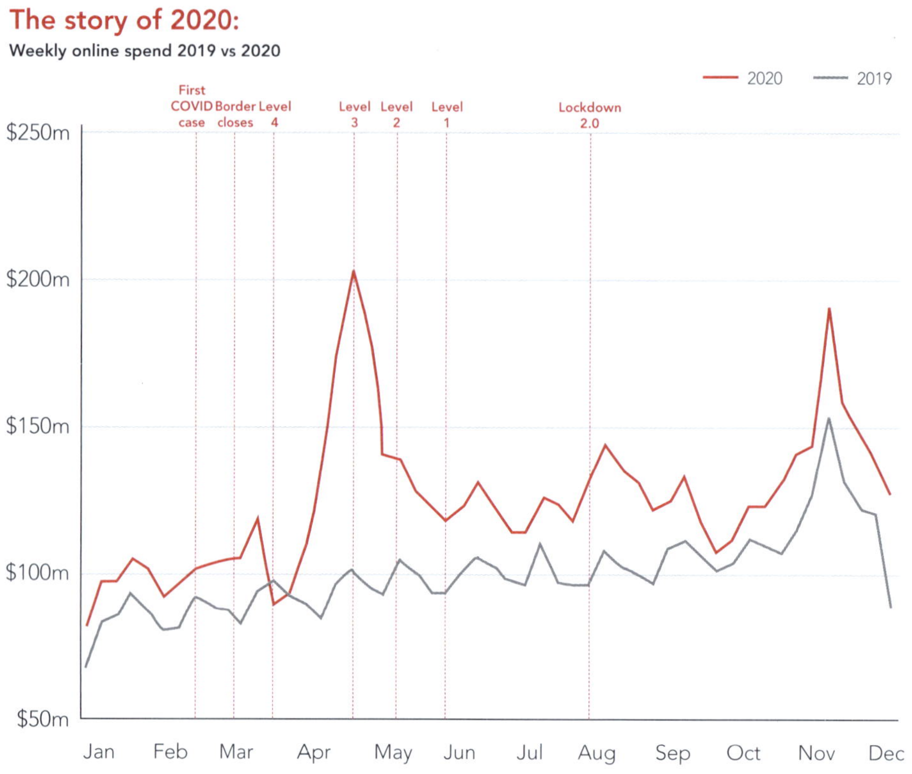

The story of 2020:
Weekly online spend 2019 vs 2020

2020 2019

First COVID case | Border closes | Level 4 | Level 3 | Level 2 | Level 1 | Lockdown 2.0

$250m $200m $150m $100m $50m

Jan Feb Mar Apr May Jun Jul Aug Sep Oct Nov Dec

a What was the approximate value spent on eCommerce at the time of the first COVID case? __________

b In which month was the largest weekly online spend in 2020? __________

c What was the likely cause of this peak? __________

____

d During which month are New Zealanders generally spending the least on eCommerce? __________

e Why might this be? __________

f 'In the week of Alert Level 3, nearly three times as much was spent on eCommerce compared with the same week in 2019.'

☐ Agree ☐ Disagree ☐ Can't tell for sure

Explain your answer.

____

____

ISBN: 9780170451833

3 NZ on Air and the Broadcasting Standards Authority analysed the use by tamariki of media in 2020.

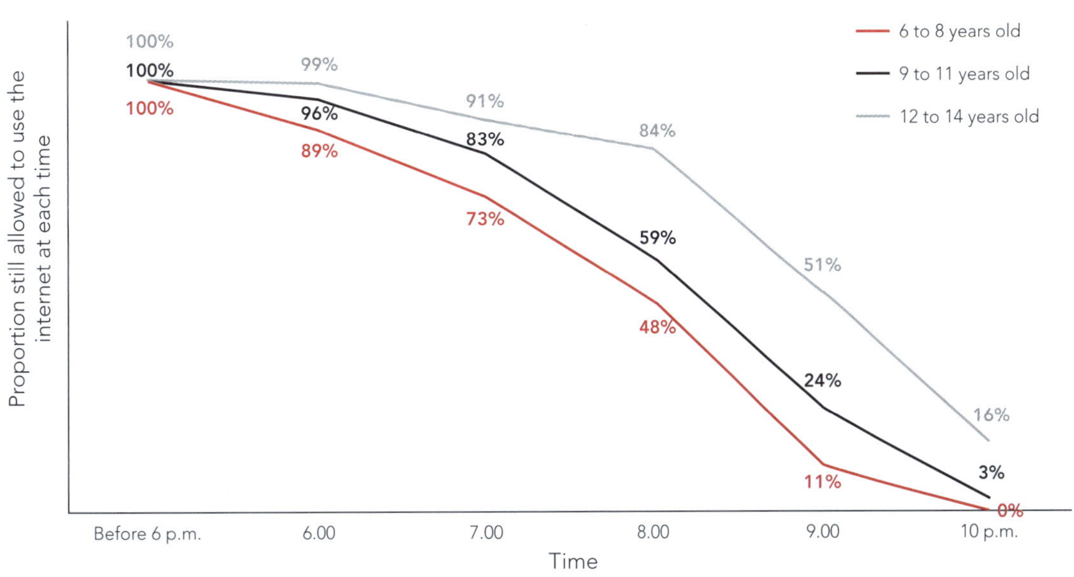

a What percentage of 12–14 year olds are allowed to use the internet at 9.00 p.m.? __________

b At what time is only 24% of 9–11 year olds allowed to use the internet? __________

c What percentage of 6–8 year olds are stopped from using the internet by 8 p.m.? __________

d How else could this data have been displayed? __________

e 'Most 12–14 year olds are allowed to access the internet after 8 p.m.'

☐ Agree ☐ Disagree ☐ Can't tell for sure

Explain your answer.

____

____

f 'Of the New Zealand 9–11 year olds 84% have been stopped from accessing the internet by 10 p.m.'

☐ Agree ☐ Disagree ☐ Can't tell for sure

Explain your answer.

____

____

ISBN: 9780170451833

Histograms

- Histograms are used to display **continuous** (**measured**) data.
- The data is displayed in **intervals**.
- There are **no gaps** between the bars.
- Histograms are used to plot the data obtained from answers to a **summative question**.

Understanding histograms

Example: This shows the mean temperature in June from 28 New Zealand locations.

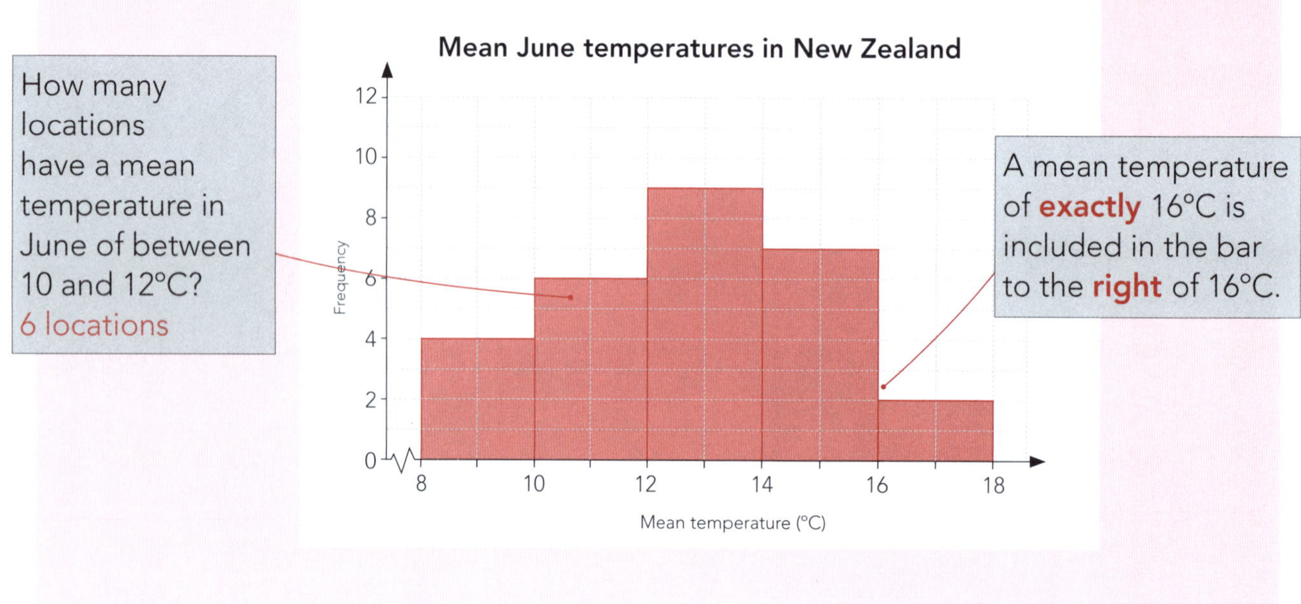

Answer the following questions. Round any calculations to 3 sf.

1 Statistics New Zealand collects data on the number of births each year. The histogram shows how many of the 58 668 births during 2021 were to mothers in each age group.

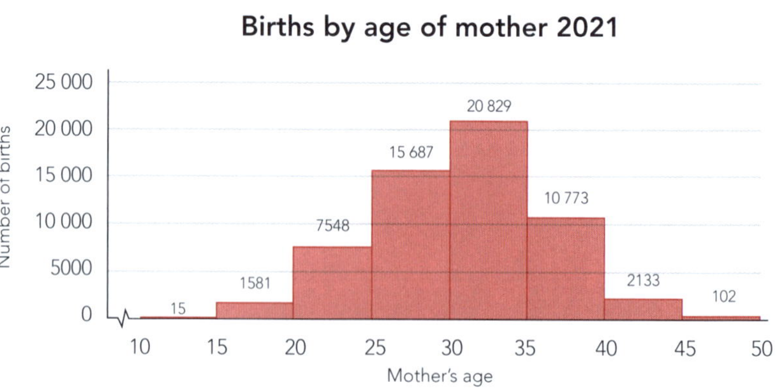

a How many babies were born to mothers between 40 and 45 years old? ____________

b What is the probability that a baby born in 2021 has a mother aged between 20 and 25? ____________

ISBN: 9780170451833

2 This shows the number of ACC claims for the 6922 e-scooter related injuries during 2018.

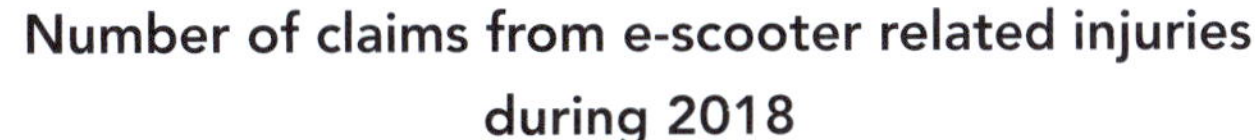
Number of claims from e-scooter related injuries during 2018

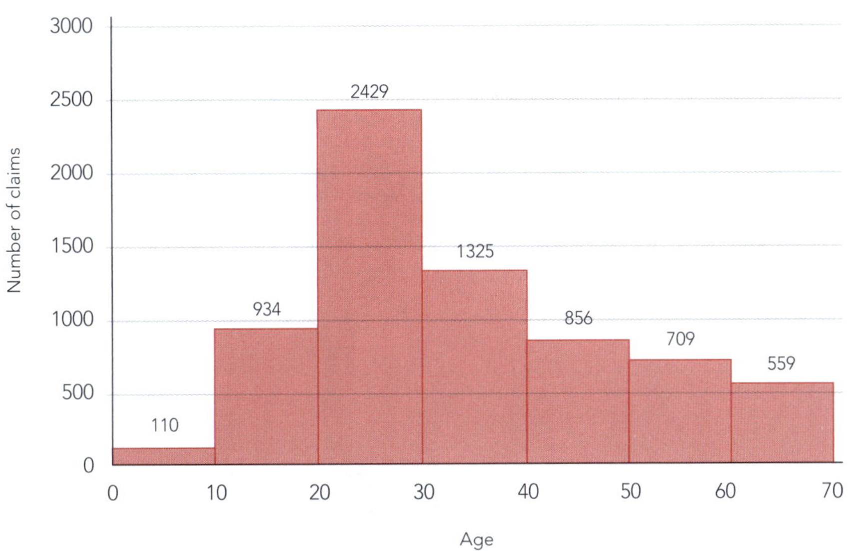

a Suggest a question that this data could be used to answer.

____

b What type of question is this? ____________

c Which age group accounts for about 35% of claims? ____________

d What percentage of claims were from people under 30 years old? ____________

e If five more 60 year olds were added to the data, write the new totals for the last two columns on the graph. ____________

ACC has paid out $16 680 910 for these claims.

f On average, how much did each claim cost? ____________

g 'E-scooters are dangerous.'

☐ Agree ☐ Disagree ☐ Can't tell for sure

Explain your answer.

____

____

ISBN: 9780170451833

3 This graph shows the ages of people who died in 1952 and 2021. The data was collected by Statistics New Zealand.

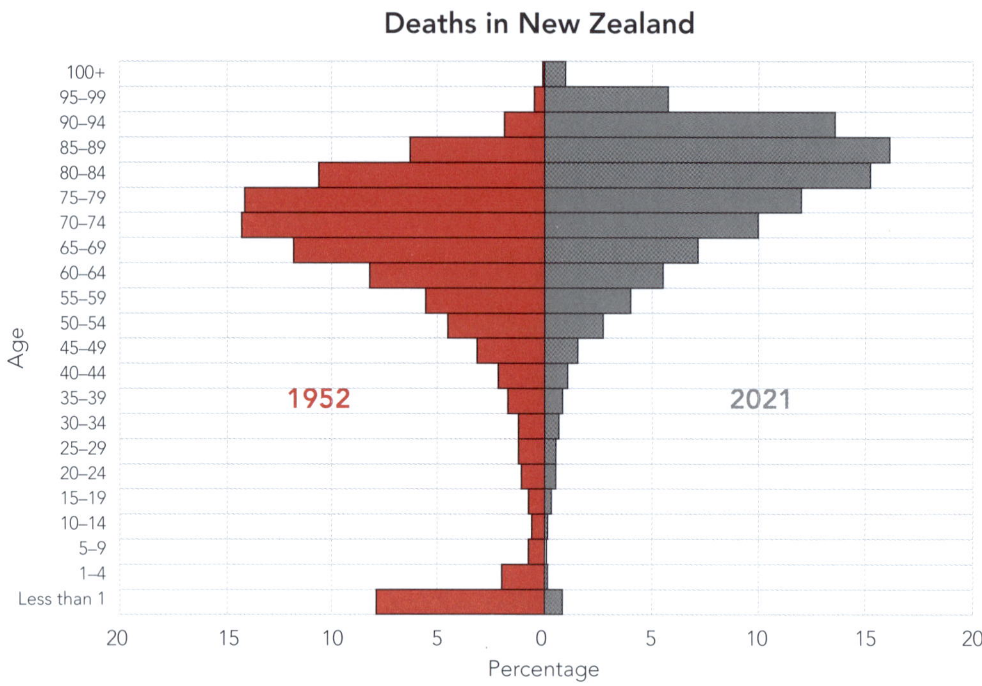

a In 1952, which age interval contained the largest proportion of deaths? __________

b In 2021, just over 15% of people died in what age range? __________

c Estimate the probability that a person dying in 2021 is over 90. __________

d There were 17 413 deaths in New Zealand in 1952. Estimate the number of children and babies under 4 years old who died during that year. __________

e 'No one lived to 100 in New Zealand in 1952.'

☐ Agree ☐ Disagree ☐ Can't tell for sure

Explain your answer.

____

____

f Describe the two biggest changes between 1952 and 2021 that this data shows.

1 ____________________

2 ____________________

ISBN: 9780170451833

Dot plots

- Dot plots are used for **discrete** and **rounded continuous** data.
- They can be useful to compare groups.
- Each dot represents one person/object, unless you are told otherwise.
- **Single** dot plots are used to plot the data obtained from answers to a **summative question**.
- **Pairs** of dot plots are used to plot the data obtained from answers to a **comparative question**.

Dot plots are useful for comparing several data sets.

Example: Heights of Year 11 and 13 students.

How many Year 11 students are 180 cm or taller? 10 students

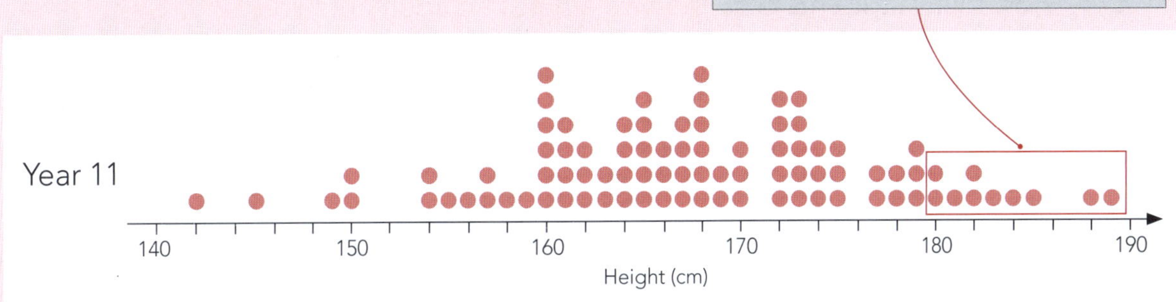

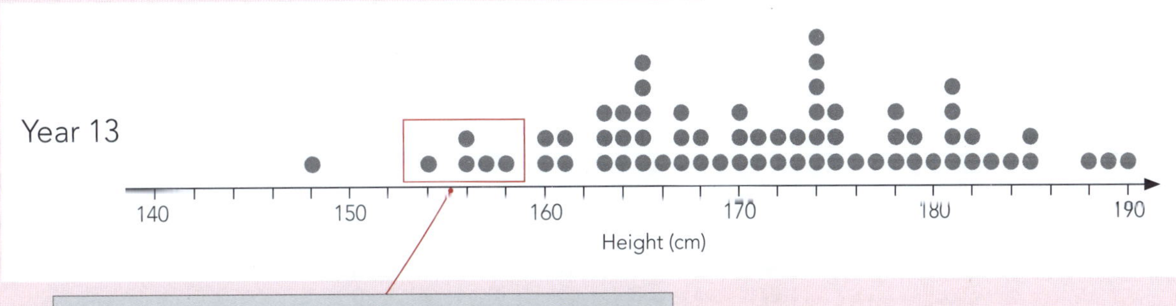

How many Year 13 students are over 150 cm and less than 160 cm? 5 students

1 Suggest a question that this data could be used to answer.

What is the difference in the heights of Year 11 students and Year 13 students?

2 What type of question is this? Comparative

3 Which year group is taller? Year 13 students

Explain your answer.

There are more dots towards the right in the Year 13 dot plot.

ISBN: 9780170451833

Answer the following questions. Round any calculations to 3 sf.

1 Thirty Year 10 students were asked 'What age do you have to reach in order to be an adult?' Their responses are shown on the dot plot.

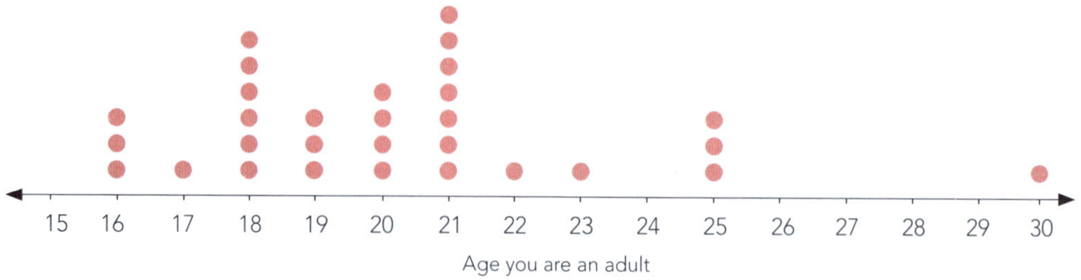

a What type of question is this? __________

b How many students thought somebody can be an adult before they turn 20? __________

c How many students consider you are not an adult until you are at least 21? __________

d What is the probability that a student thought a 16 year old is an adult? __________

2 Two restaurants were given scores out of 10 for their customer service.

Restaurant A

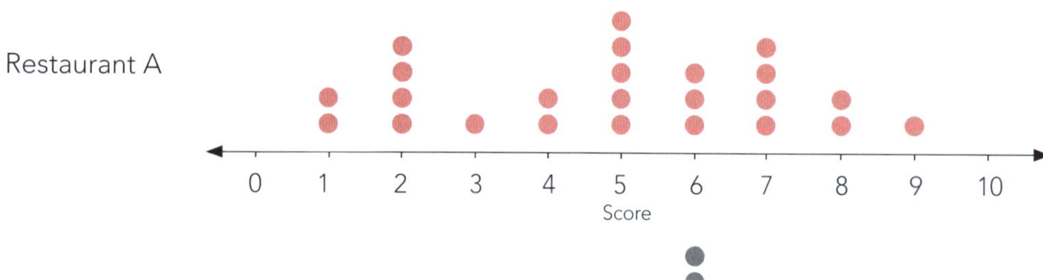

Restaurant B

0 1 2 3 4 5 6 7 8 9 10
Score

a How many customers gave restaurant B at least a 6? __________

b Which restaurant had the most variable service? __________

Explain your answer. ______________________________

c 'Customers at restaurant B were more satisfied with the customer service than those who went to restaurant A.'

☐ Agree ☐ Disagree ☐ Can't tell for sure

Explain your answer. ______________________________

____

ISBN: 9780170451833

3 These graphs show the number of beds in all the Department of Conservation standard huts in Otago and in Hawke's Bay.

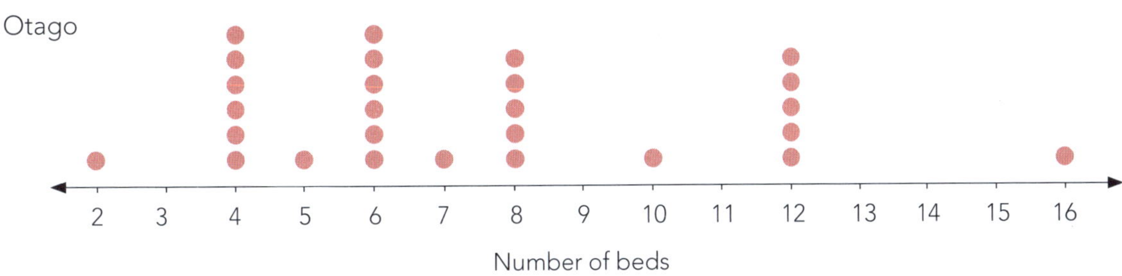

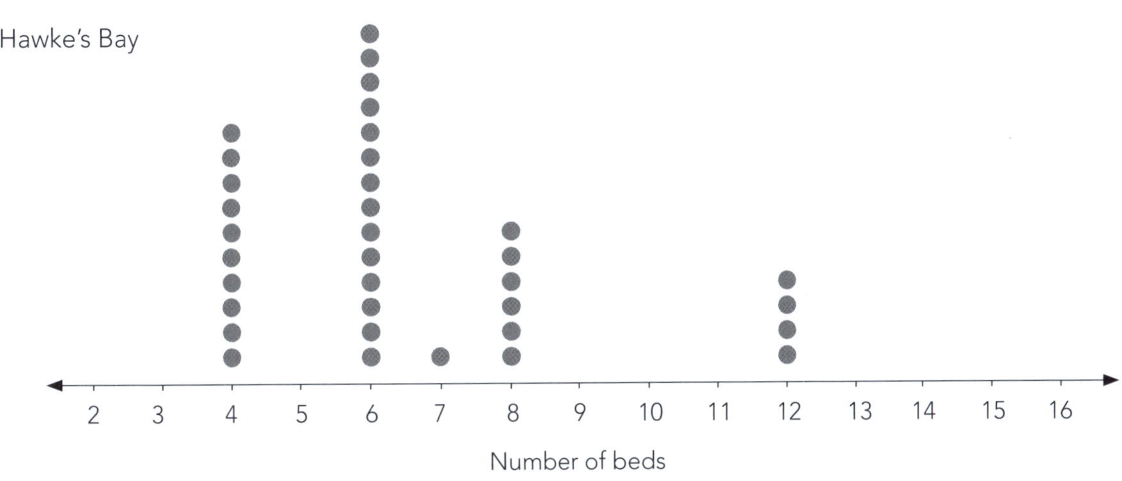

a Which region has the hut with the largest number of beds? __________

b If a hut in Hawke's Bay was selected at random, what's the probability that it sleeps 12? __________

c What percentage of huts in Otago can sleep more than eight people? __________

d 'The number of beds in standard huts in Otago is more variable than those in Hawke's Bay.'

☐ Agree ☐ Disagree ☐ Can't tell for sure

Explain your answer. __________

____

e 'There are more beds in DOC huts for trampers in Hawke's Bay than in Otago.'

☐ Agree ☐ Disagree ☐ Can't tell for sure

Explain your answer. __________

____

ISBN: 9780170451833

Describing features of dot plots

Spread

This can be calculated or compared.

Shape

If samples are large enough, you may be able to comment on the shape.
None will be perfect, so use the term '**tends towards**'.

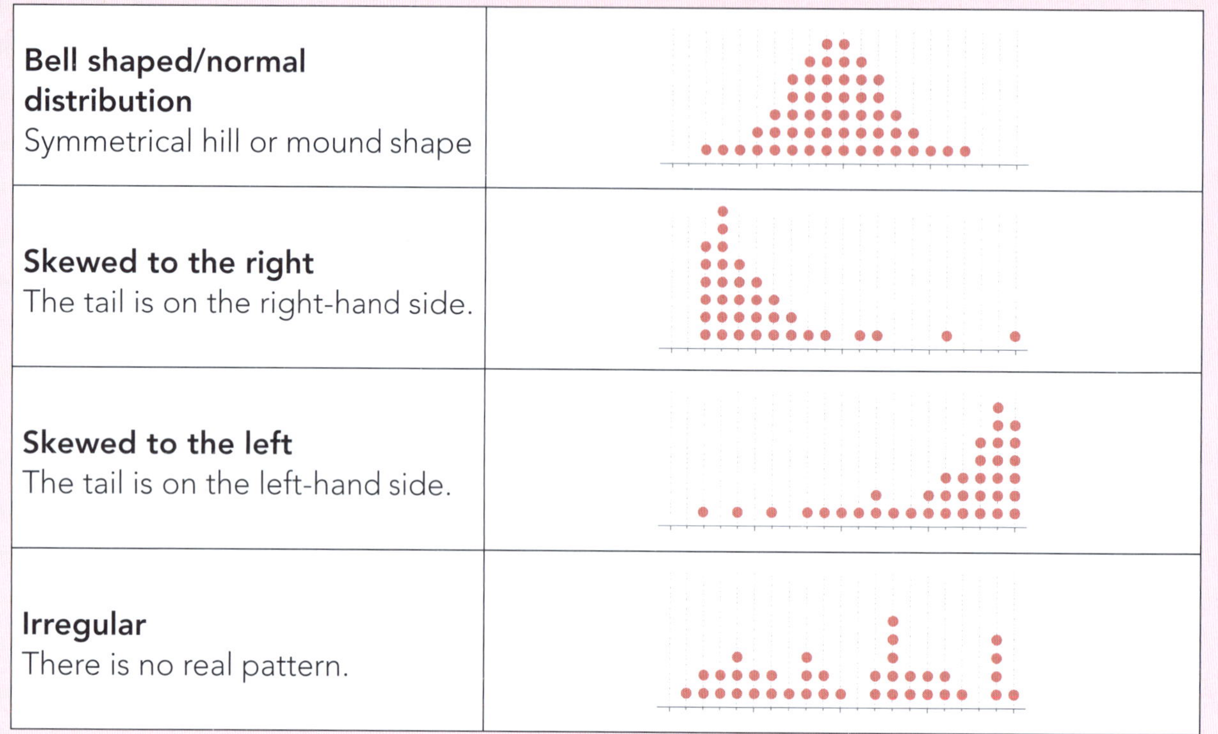

Bell shaped/normal distribution Symmetrical hill or mound shape	
Skewed to the right The tail is on the right-hand side.	
Skewed to the left The tail is on the left-hand side.	
Irregular There is no real pattern.	

Highlight the shape that these graphs tend towards.

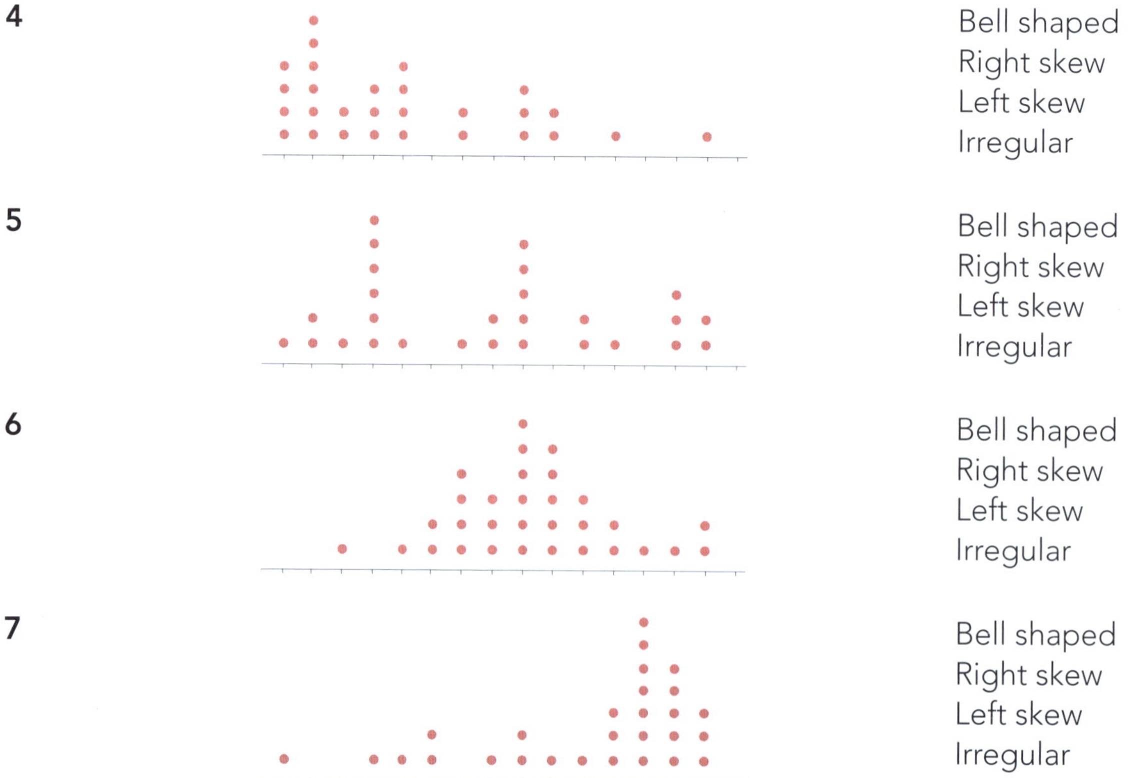

4

Bell shaped
Right skew
Left skew
Irregular

5

Bell shaped
Right skew
Left skew
Irregular

6

Bell shaped
Right skew
Left skew
Irregular

7

Bell shaped
Right skew
Left skew
Irregular

 ISBN: 9780170451833

Scatter plots

- A scatter plot is used to show the **relationship** between **two variables**.
- These variables can be **continuous** or **discrete**.
- Each dot represents two pieces of data about one object, e.g. the height and mass of a person.
- Scatter plots are used to show data obtained from **relationship questions**.

Coordinates revision

- A positive **x** coordinate tells you how far to move to the **right**.
- A positive **y** coordinate tells you how far to move **up**.
- Coordinates are written in brackets, in alphabetical order: **(x, y)**.

Understanding scatter plots

Examples:

1 This graph shows the heights and bag masses of some New Zealand secondary school students.

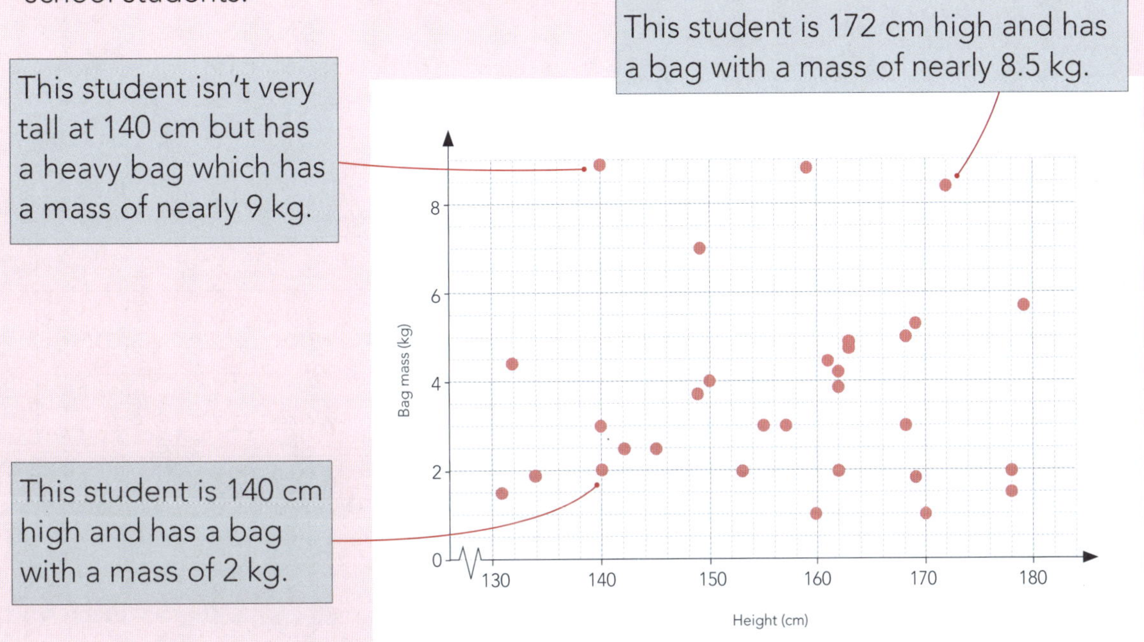

2 Scatter graphs can also be interpreted without numbers.

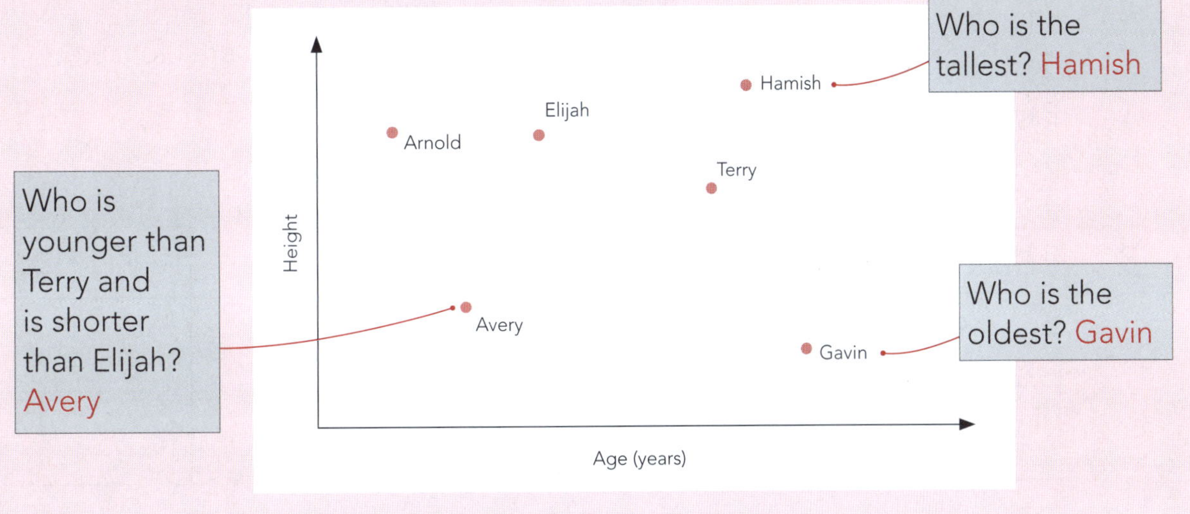

ISBN: 9780170451833

1 Xiu plotted the temperature and the number of visitors to the beach.

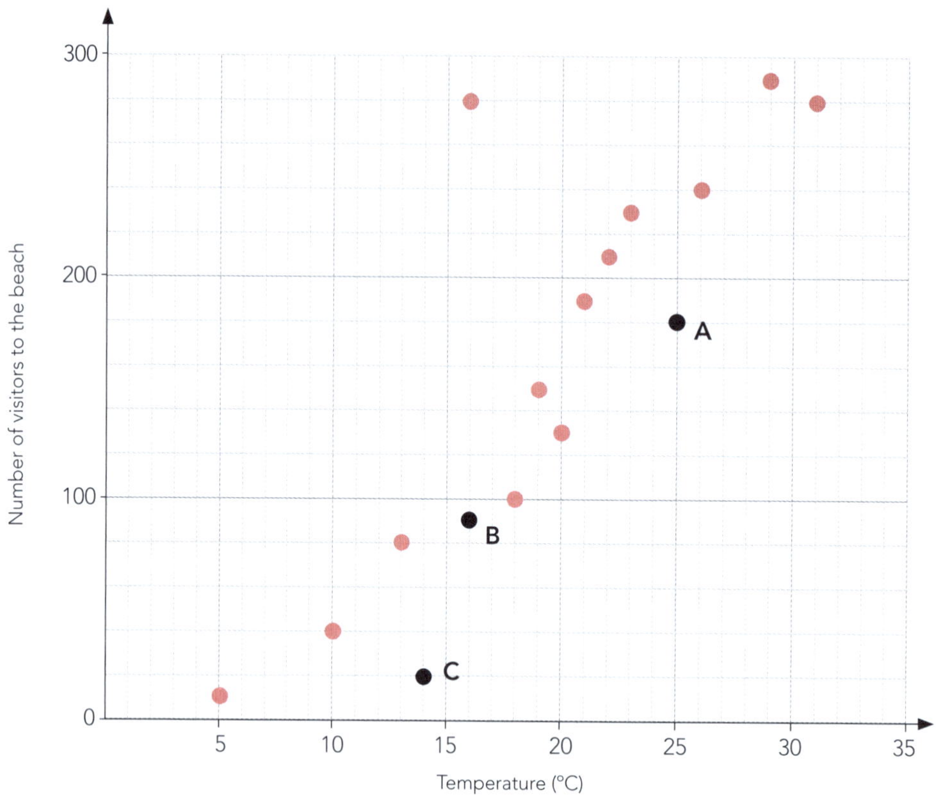

a

Day	Coordinates	Description
A	(______, ______)	It was ______°C and there were ______ visitors.
B	(______, ______)	It was ______°C and there were ______ visitors.
C	(______, ______)	It was ______°C and there were ______ visitors.

b One day was unusual. Describe it.

____

c 'People don't go to the beach if it's cold.'

☐ Agree ☐ Disagree ☐ Can't tell for sure

Explain your answer. ____

____

d

	Do you agree with these statements?	✓ or ✗
i	As the number of visitors decreases, the temperature drops.	
ii	As the temperature increases, more visitors tend to come to the beach.	

ISBN: 9780170451833

2 The time spent studying for a mathematics test and the grades received were recorded.

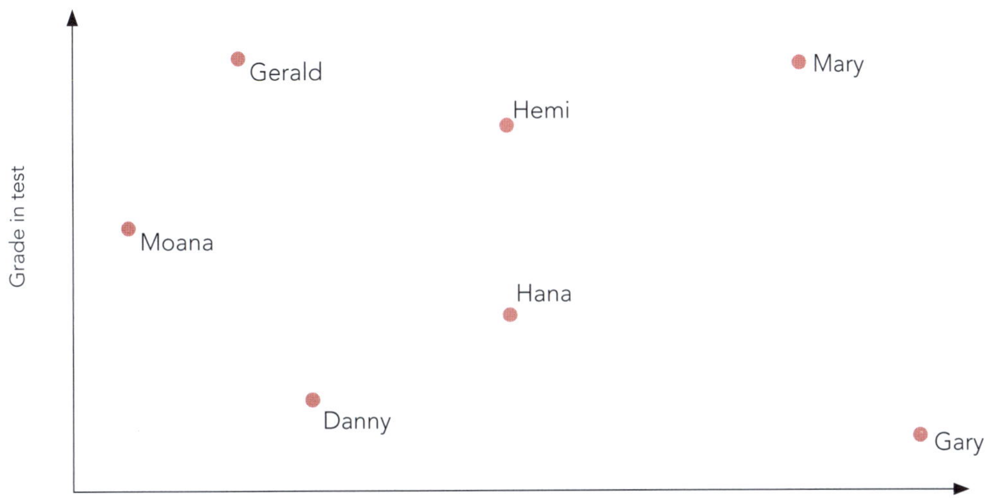

Are these statements true or false?

a Hana spent less time studying than Gary, but got a better grade. True/False

b Mary spent the most time studying and got one of the highest grades. True/False

c Hemi spent more time studying than Gerald, but got a lower grade. True/False

d Danny spent more time studying than Moana and did better than she did. True/False

e Gerald spent longer studying than Hemi and got a better grade. True/False

f 'Gary is not very good at mathematics.'

☐ Agree ☐ Disagree ☐ Can't tell for sure

Explain your answer. ____________________

____

g 'The graph suggest that Gerald is good at mathematics.'

☐ Agree ☐ Disagree ☐ Can't tell for sure

Explain your answer. ____________________

____

ISBN: 9780170451833

Describing and comparing features of scatter plots

Direction

Positive:

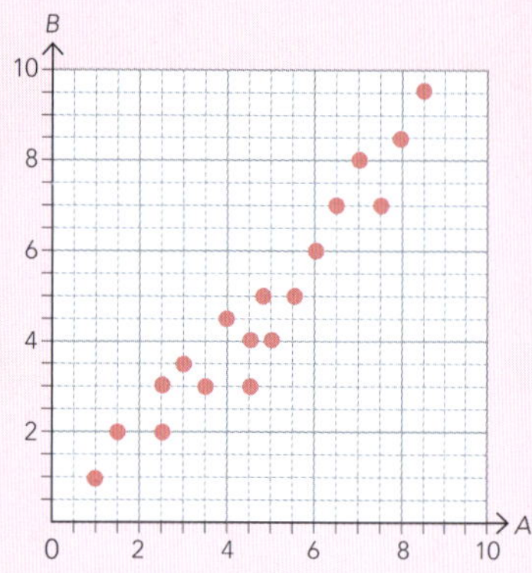

As *A* gets bigger, *B* gets **bigger**.

Negative:

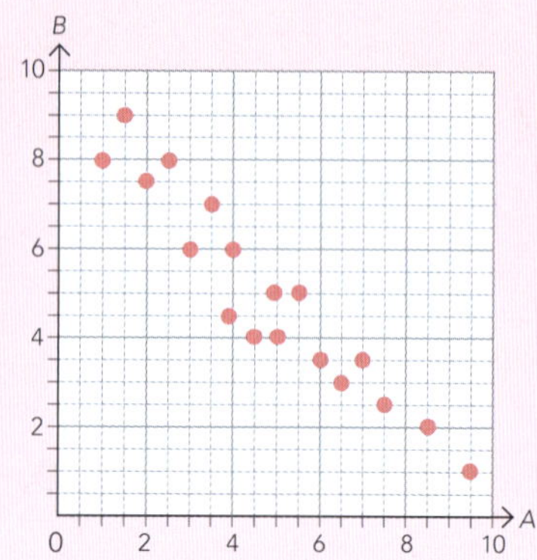

As *A* gets bigger, *B* gets **smaller**.

Strength

Strong:

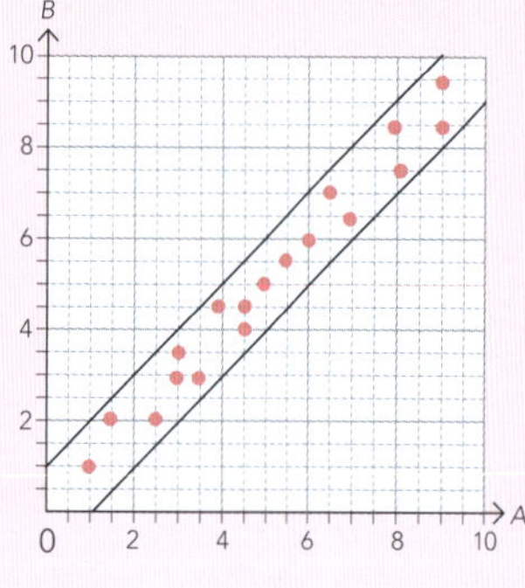

This means:

- You can have confidence that the relationship is strong.

Moderate:

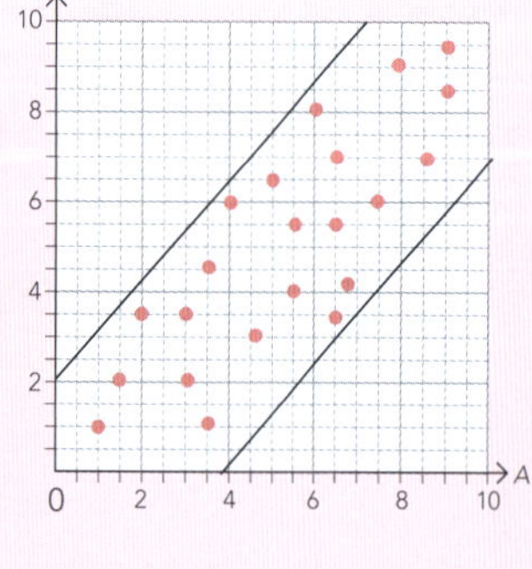

This means:

- The relationship is moderately strong.

Weak:

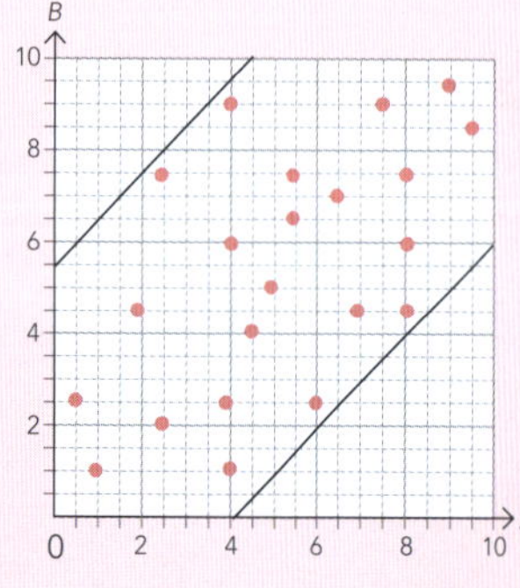

This means:

- The relationship is weak.

ISBN: 9780170451833

Write the appropriate descriptors for these graphs.

3

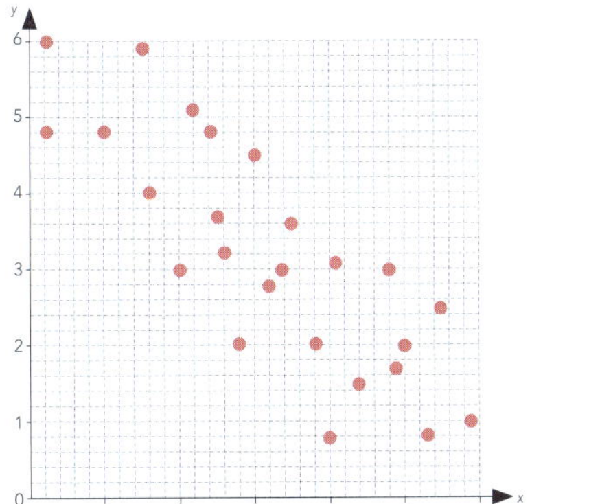

Direction: ______________________

Strength: ______________________

4

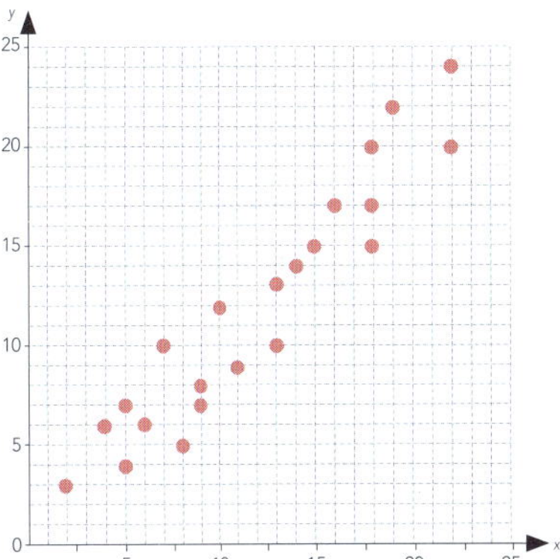

Direction: ______________________

Strength: ______________________

5

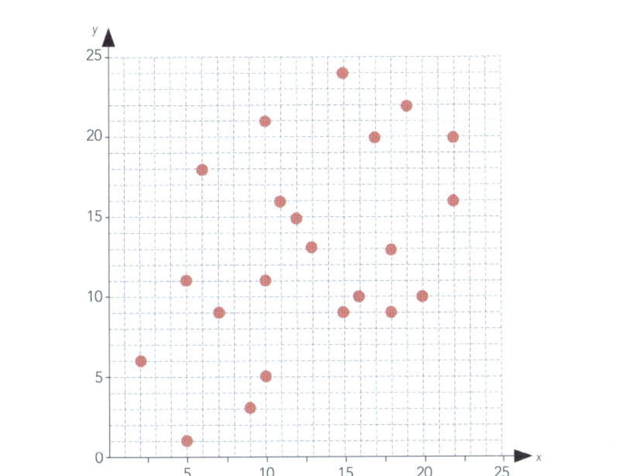

Direction: ______________________

Strength: ______________________

6

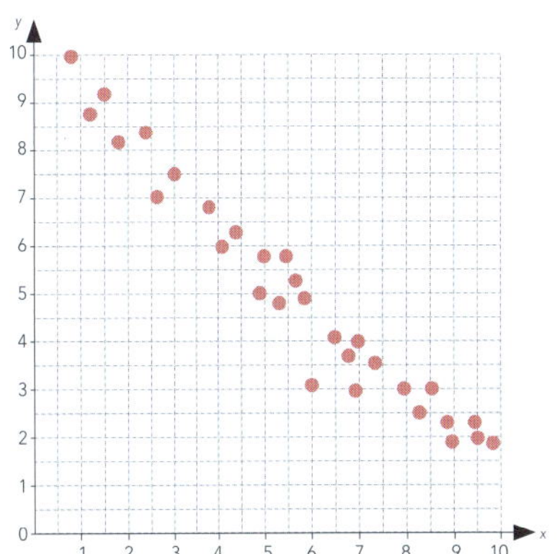

Direction: ______________________

Strength: ______________________

7

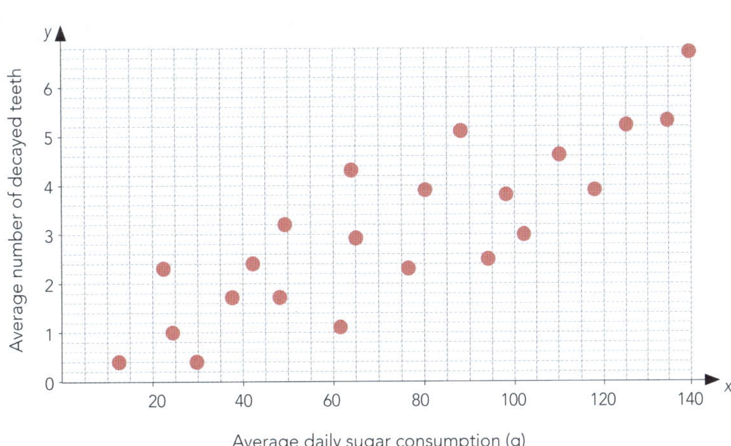

The graph shows a positive/negative relationship between sugar consumption and the average number of decayed teeth. This suggests that people who consume more sugar tend to have ______________________ decayed teeth.

ISBN: 9780170451833

Statistical tables

- Tables are often used when there is a lot of data or it is complicated.

Example: Companion Animal New Zealand regularly undertakes surveys to collect data on the companion animal population.

New Zealand companion animal population breakdown, 2020

Companion animal type	Percentage of households with animal type	Average number in home	Total (000)
Birds	6%	5.2	560
Cats	41%	17	1219
Dogs	34%	1.4	851
Fish	9%	8.1	1368
Horses/ponies	1.6%	2.5	72
Rabbits	2.8%	2.4	121
Other small mammal	1.8%	3.2	101
Reptile	1.3%	2.6	60
Total	**64%**	–	**4352**

What percentage of homes have a rabbit? 2.8%

How many pet reptiles are in New Zealand? 60,000

Answer the following questions. Round any calculations to 3 sf.

1 This data is from Surf Life Saving NZ.

Year	Total drownings	Beach drownings	Percentage
2020/21	42	11	26%
2019/20	55	18	33%
2018/19	55	16	29%
2017/18	58	14	24%

a How many beach drownings were there in 2018/19? ____________

b What percentage of total drownings in 2020/21 were not beach drownings? ____________

c 'The number of beach drownings each year in New Zealand is decreasing.'

☐ Agree ☐ Disagree ☐ Can't tell for sure

Explain your answer. ____

____

 ISBN: 9780170451833

2 Sport New Zealand did a survey in 2019 regarding how active New Zealanders are.

Average time spent per week participating in organised and informal sports and activities by age (hours)

2019	Total	5–7	8–11	12–14	15–17
Organised					
Physical education or class at school	2.1	1.9 ▼	2.2	2.8 ▲	1.3 ▼
Competition or tournament	0.8	0.2 ▼	0.6 ▼	1.4 ▲	0.8
Training or practising with a coach	1.7	0.8 ▼	1.5 ▼	2.4 ▲	2.0 ▲
Informal					
Playing or hanging out with friends or family	4.3	5.6 ▲	4.6 ▲	4.3	2.4 ▲
Playing on your own	1.6	2.2 ▲	1.7	1.5	1.1 ▼
Extra exercise, training, practice with a coach or instructor	0.7	0.1 ▼	0.2 ▼	1.2 ▲	1.4 ▲
Total time	**10.9**	**10.8**	**10.7**	**12.8 ▲**	**8.7 ▼**
Organised combined	4.6	2.9 ▼	4.3 ▼	6.6	4.0 ▼
Informal combined	6.5	7.9 ▲	6.5	6.8	4.7 ▼

'Total' means the mean time for all four age groups.

▲▼ Significantly higher/lower than total
Base: All respondents age 5 to 17

a On average, how many hours a week are 5–7 year olds playing on their own? ____________

b On average, how many hours a week are 12–14 year olds involved in organised activity? ____________

c On average, how many hours a week in total are 15–17 year olds in a competition or tournament? ____________

d 'Younger children are more likely to play on their own.'

☐ Agree ☐ Disagree ☐ Can't tell for sure

Explain your answer. ____

____

e 'Informal activity is more common than organised activity.'

☐ Agree ☐ Disagree ☐ Can't tell for sure

Explain your answer. ____

____

ISBN: 9780170451833

3 ACC compiles data on types of claims each year.

Sports claims and costs by year

Year	New claims	Active claims	Cost of active claims
2015	487,868	548,608	$508,625,110
2016	499,485	566,939	$542,263,593
2017	484,545	554,510	$569,274,166
2018	467,867	546,041	$611,121,240
2019	455,292	537,080	$620,094,191
2020	402,532	485,863	$631,877,509
2021	417,488	507,212	$692,718,070

a How many new claims were there in 2021? ____________

b In which year did active claims cost the most? ____________

c How many claims were there in total in 2019? ____________

d 'People are getting hurt less in the most recent years.'

☐ Agree ☐ Disagree ☐ Can't tell for sure

Explain your answer. ____

____

e 'The cost is increasing, so people must be receiving worse injuries.'

☐ Agree ☐ Disagree ☐ Can't tell for sure

Explain your answer. ____

____

 ISBN: 9780170451833

4 This is another set of data from Companion Animal New Zealand.

Companion animal	Percentage of households with animal type			Average number in home			Total (000)		
	2011	2015	2020	2011	2015	2020	2011	2015	2020
Birds	6%	7%	6%	4.9	5.4	5.2	527	595	560
Cats	48%	44%	41%	1.8	1.5	1.7	1,419	1,134	1,219
Dogs	29%	28%	34%	1.5	1.4	1.4	700	683	851
Fish	11%	10%	9%	9.1	8.9	8.7	1,678	1,510	1,368
Horses/ponies	2%	2%	1.6%	3.2	3.4	2.5	87	116	72
Rabbits	3%	3%	2.8%	1.7	2.0	2.4	88	116	121
Other small mammal	–	–	1.8%	–	–	3.2	–	–	101
Reptile	–	–	1.3%	–	–	2.6	–	–	60
Total	**68%**	**64%**	**64%**	**–**	**–**	**–**	**4,945**	**4,656**	**4,352**

a What was the percentage of households with dogs in 2011? __________

b What was the average number of fish in homes in 2015? __________

c How many cats were there in 2020? __________

d The total number of household companions is increasing/decreasing.

e 'Fish are a more popular pet than dogs.'

☐ Agree ☐ Disagree ☐ Can't tell for sure

Explain your answer. __________

____

f 'Cats aren't as popular as they used to be.'

☐ Agree ☐ Disagree ☐ Can't tell for sure

Explain your answer. __________

____

ISBN: 9780170451833

Infographics

- Infographics are modifications of traditional graphs or diagrams used to convey numerical information.
- They are often visually pleasing, but they don't always make the message clearer.

Answer the following questions. Round any calculations to 3 sf.

1 Read New Zealand conducted a study in 2021 about reading habits of New Zealand adults. This infographic displays the types of books that are being read.

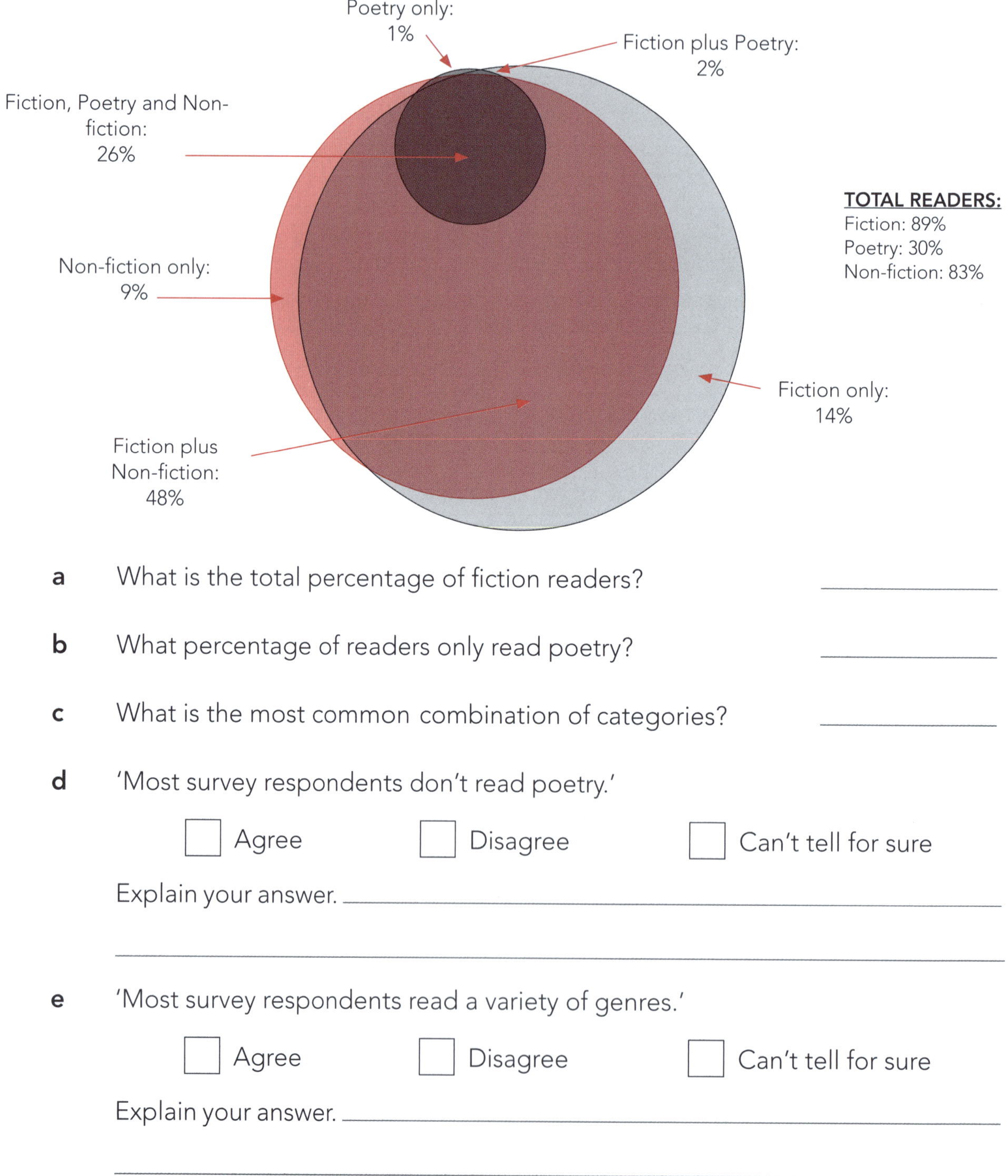

a What is the total percentage of fiction readers? ______________

b What percentage of readers only read poetry? ______________

c What is the most common combination of categories? ______________

d 'Most survey respondents don't read poetry.'

☐ Agree ☐ Disagree ☐ Can't tell for sure

Explain your answer. ____

____

e 'Most survey respondents read a variety of genres.'

☐ Agree ☐ Disagree ☐ Can't tell for sure

Explain your answer. ____

____

 ISBN: 9780170451833

2 Thousands of items are flushed down toilets every day in New Zealand. This infographic shows what people think happens to baby wipes and cotton bud sticks.

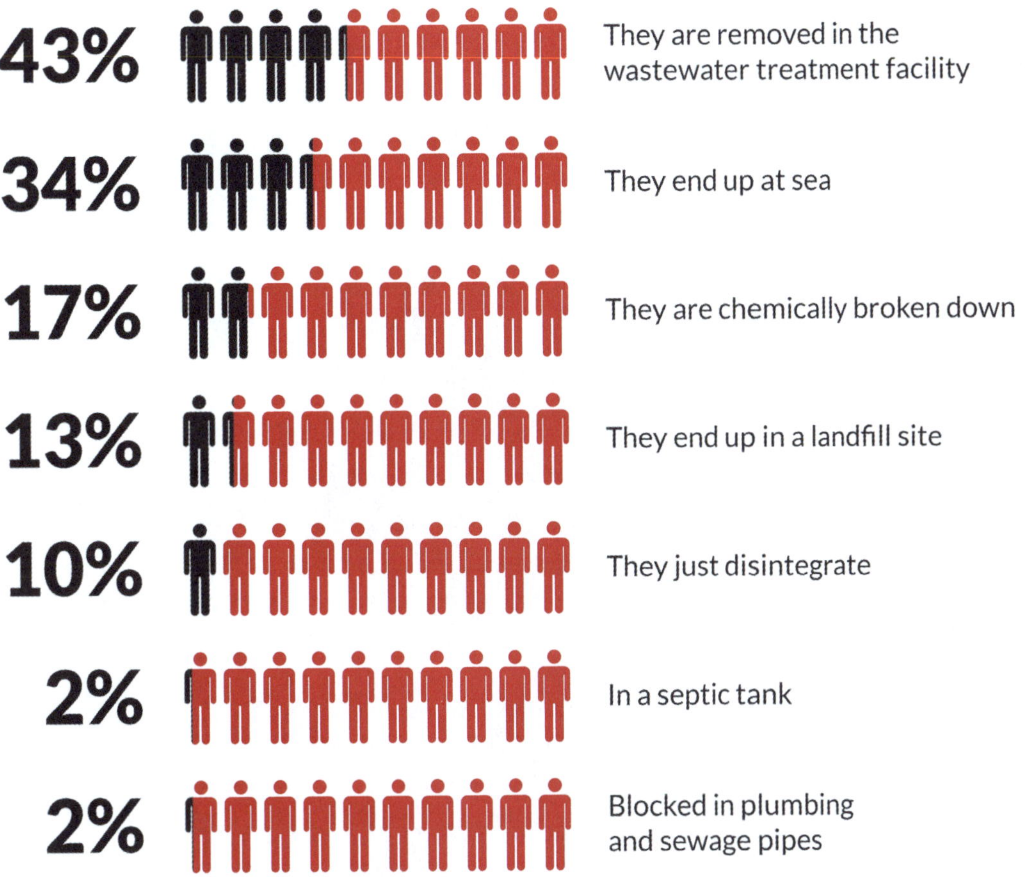

a What is the most common belief about what happens to these items?

____

b What percentage of adults think that they are chemically broken down? _______________

c If we apply these findings to the adult population of New Zealand (approximately 4 million), how many of these adults think that these items end up at sea? _______________

d Three in ten of the 4 million adults have flushed things that shouldn't be flushed. Approximately how many adults in New Zealand are guilty of this? _______________

e In practice, these things usually end up blocking plumbing and sewage pipes. Approximately how many adults realise this? _______________

ISBN: 9780170451833

3 Companion Animal New Zealand regularly undertakes surveys to collect data on the companion animal (pet) population.

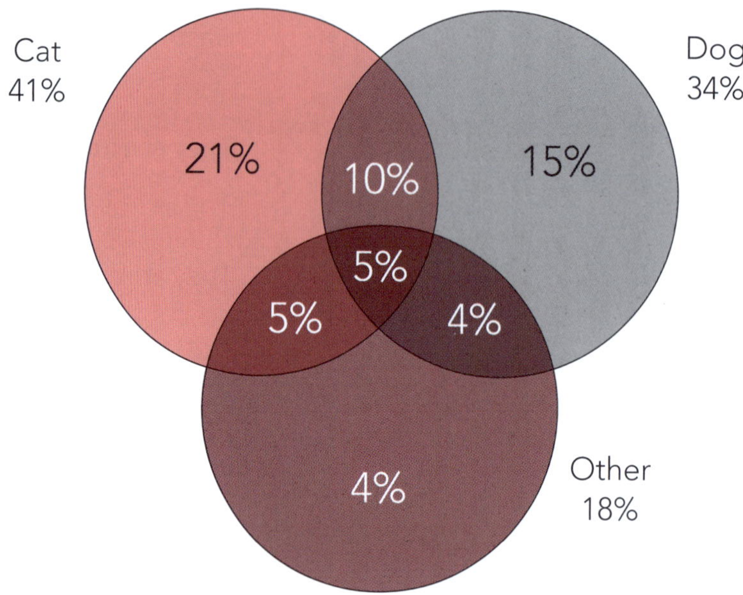

a What percentage of households have just a cat? ____________

b What percentage of households have a cat and dog? ____________

c What percentage of households have a pet that is neither a cat nor a dog? ____________

d What percentage of households have no companion animals? ____________

4 NZ Post annually reviews the eCommerce in New Zealand. The graph (see following page) shows the amount spent, annual growth in spending, number of transactions, basket size (value of each transaction) and growth in basket size in 2020.

a How much did Northland online shoppers spend in 2020? ____________

b How many transactions did Gisborne residents make in 2020? ____________

c What is the average basket size of Taranaki shoppers? ____________

d How fast is eCommerce growing in Hawke's Bay? ____________

e Which region has the most rapid growth in basket size? ____________

ISBN: 9780170451833

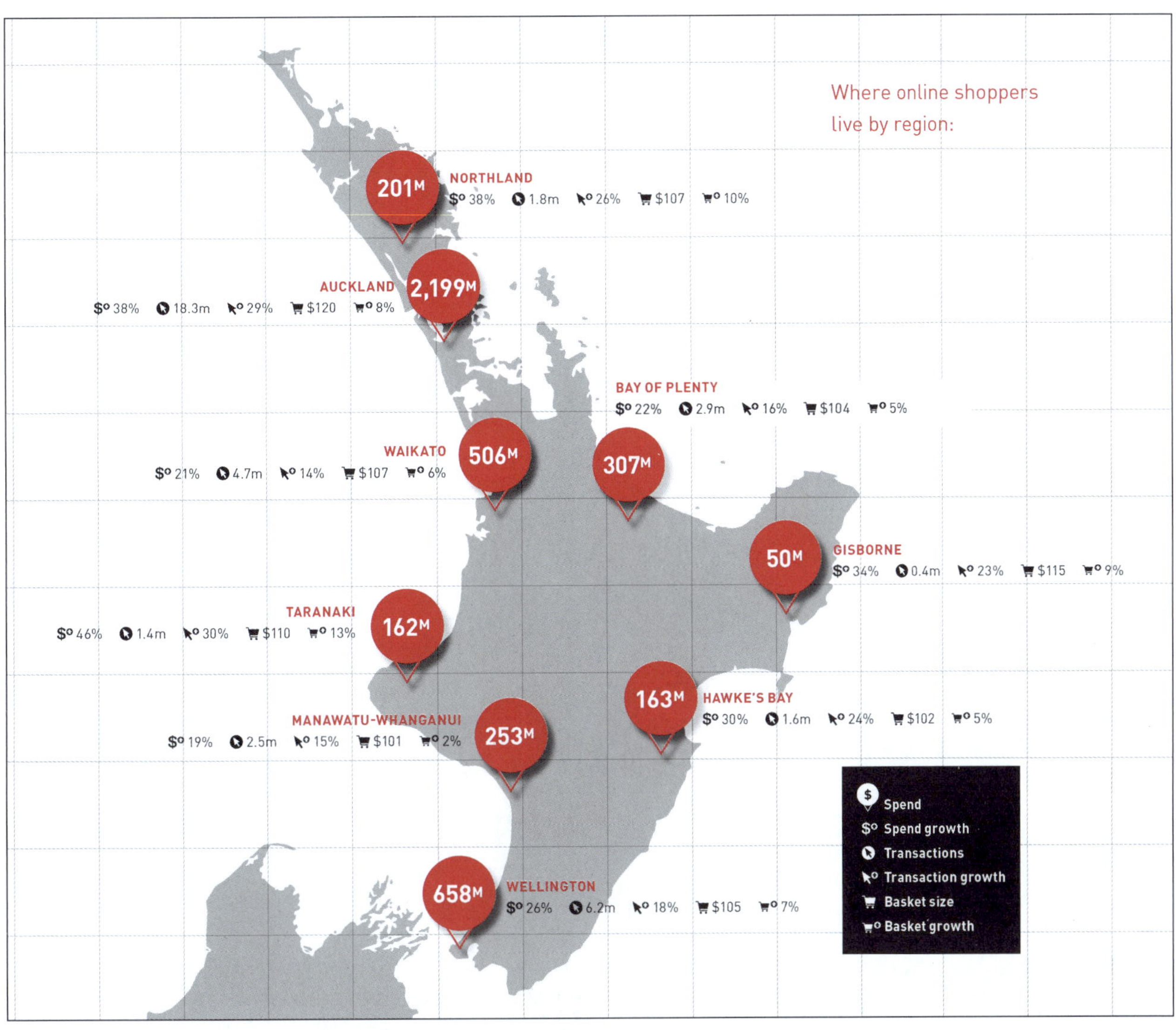

f 'Wellington e-Commerce shoppers are spending more than those from the Waikato.'

☐ Agree ☐ Disagree ☐ Can't tell for sure

Explain your answer. ______________________________

____

g 'Bay of Plenty shoppers are spending on average a similar amount to those in the Taranaki.'

☐ Agree ☐ Disagree ☐ Can't tell for sure

Explain your answer. ______________________________

____

ISBN: 9780170451833

5 This infographic has been made using data from the 2018 census. It describes the population as if New Zealand had 100 people in total: 80 adults (over 15 years) and 20 children.

These are the occupations of the 52 adults who are employed:

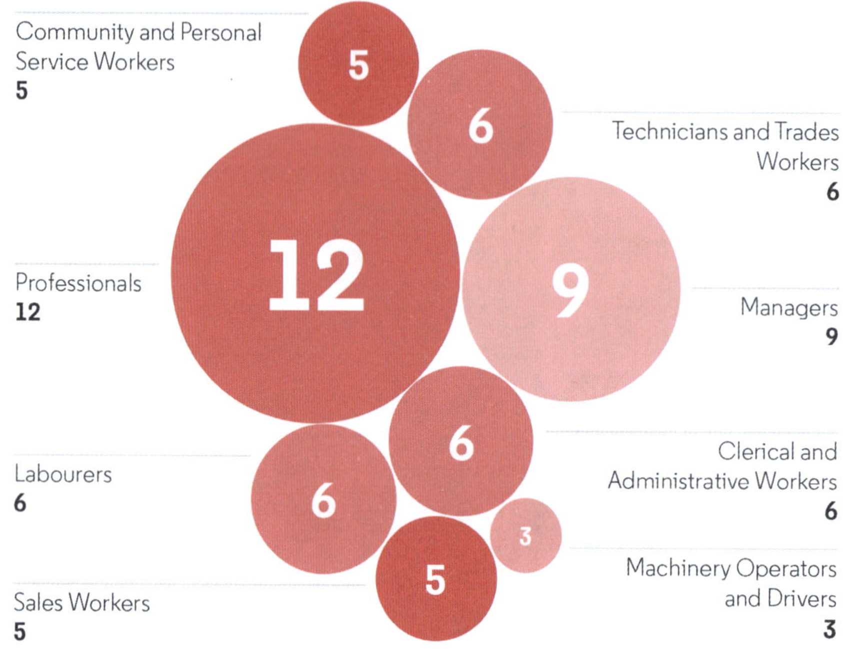

a What percentage of New Zealand adults were 'professionals'? __________

b What percentage of those described as 'workers' were sales workers? __________

c New Zealand had an adult population of around 3.9 million in 2018. How many of them would you expect to be managers? __________

Additional information:

- 40 people in our village were employed full-time (16 women and 24 men)
- 12 people were employed part-time (8 women and 4 men)
- 3 people were unemployed (2 women and 1 man)
- 25 people were not in the labour force (15 women and 10 men).

d Based on this information, which of these statements are true?

☐ Men were more likely to be employed than women.

☐ The probability that a randomly picked adult was a woman who is employed full-time is 0.2.

☐ The probability that a randomly picked adult was a man who is unemployed or not in the labour force is 0.211 (3 sf).

☐ The probability that a randomly picked employed adult was a man in part-time employment is 0.0769 (3 sf).

ISBN: 9780170451833

6 Statistics New Zealand created this infographic from the 2018 census information. It's depicted as if New Zealand were a village of 100 people, 80 of whom are adults. This infographic displays gender and personal income of those 80 adults.

Personal income

The incomes of people in our village...

$30,000 and less
39 people

$30,001 to **$70,000**
27 people

$70,001 to **$100,000**
8 people

$100,001 or more
6 people

Women

Men

a How many of the 80 adults are women who earn between $30 001 and $70 000? ______

b How many of the 80 adults have a personal income of $100 001 or more? ______

c What percentage of those who earn $100 001 or more are men? ______

d The New Zealand adult population is about 4 million people. Approximately how many of them are earning $30 000 or less? ______

e 'Most adults in New Zealand earn less than $70 001 a year.'

☐ Agree ☐ Disagree ☐ Can't tell for sure

Explain your answer. ______

f 'Men have higher personal incomes than women.'

☐ Agree ☐ Disagree ☐ Can't tell for sure

Explain your answer. ______

ISBN: 9780170451833

7 Statistics New Zealand graphed 2013 census information about salary and how many vehicles in households with different total incomes.

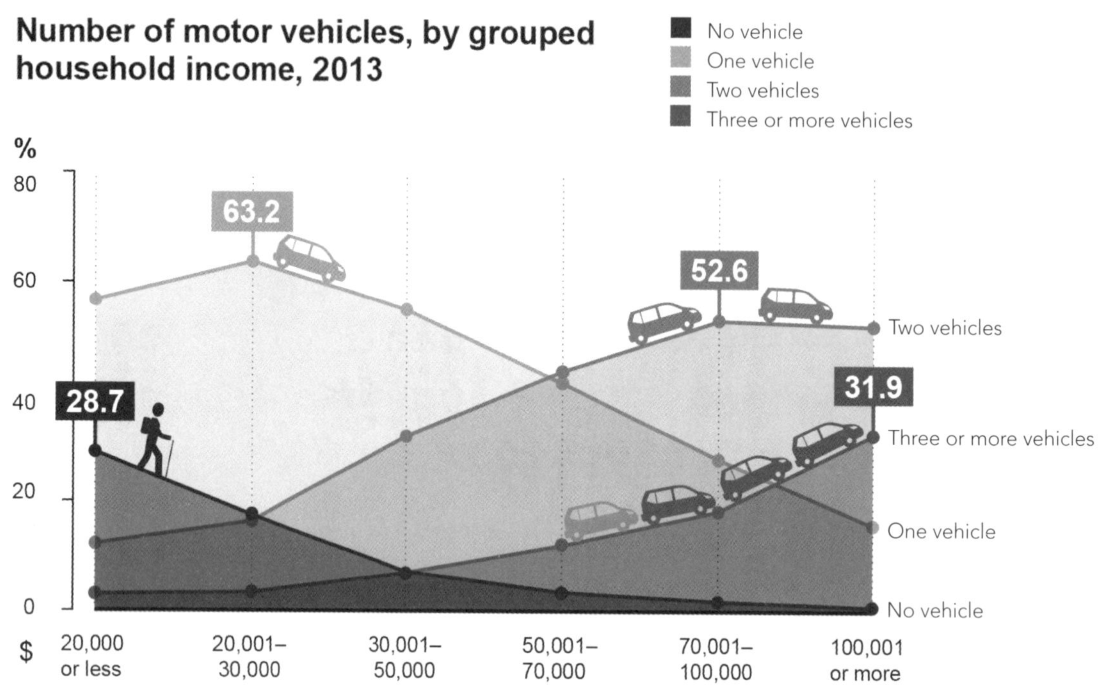

a Estimate the percentage of New Zealand households with an income of between \$20 001 and \$30 000 with no vehicle. ______

b Those who have no vehicle are most likely to be in which income category? ______

c A household with an income of between \$50 001 and \$70 000 is most likely to have how many vehicles? ______

d 'People with higher household incomes tend to have more vehicles.'

☐ Agree ☐ Disagree ☐ Can't tell for sure

Explain your answer. ______

______

e 'Every household with an income of \$100 001 or more has a vehicle.'

☐ Agree ☐ Disagree ☐ Can't tell for sure

Explain your answer. ______

______

 ISBN: 9780170451833

Data analysis

- There are two measures that we need to know in order to be able to discuss and compare distributions:
  1 Where is the **centre** of the data?
  2 How widely is the data **spread**?

Measures of centre (averages)

- There are **three** measures for the centre of data.

Name	Calculation	Advantages	Disadvantages
Mean	$\frac{\text{the sum of all the data values}}{\text{the number of data values}}$	• Easy to calculate	• Distorted by very big or small values
Median	middle value	• Usually a good measure of centre	• Data must be put in order
Mode	value that occurs most frequently	• Very easy to find	• Very unreliable as measure of centre • Often there are two or none

Mean

- The mean is sometimes falsely called the average.
- The numbers do not need to be in order for this calculation.
- Means are not always whole numbers, so sensible rounding may be needed.
- The mean is influenced by unusually large or small values.

$$\textbf{mean} = \frac{\textbf{sum of all the data values}}{\textbf{number of data values}}$$

Notice that 0 must be included in the calculation.

Example:

0 2 6 1 7 6 9 9 55

$$\text{Mean} = \frac{0 + 2 + 6 + 1 + 7 + 6 + 9 + 9 + 55}{9}$$

$$= 10.\dot{5}$$

There are 9 numbers in the data set.

The mean of this data set is $10.\dot{5}$ or 10.6 (1 dp).

Notice what happens to the mean if the 55 is removed.

0 2 6 1 7 6 9 9

$$\text{Mean} = \frac{0 + 2 + 6 + 1 + 7 + 6 + 9 + 9}{8}$$

$$= 5$$

There are now 8 numbers in the data set.

The mean of this data set is 5.

The 55 was so much larger than the other values that it influenced the mean.

ISBN: 9780170451833

Median

- If there is an **odd number of values** in a data, the median is the **middle number**.
- If there is an **even number of values**, the median is **halfway between the two middle numbers** in the data set.
- Before you can calculate the median, you must **put the data in order**.

Examples:

1 A data set with an odd number of values

11 17 10 12 18 21 25 11 14

Put them **in order** before finding the median: **10 11 11 12 14 17 18 21 25**

This is the middle number.

The median of this data set = 14.

2 A data set with an even number of values

0 0 4 4 5 8 9 9 12 14 15 17

The median for this data set = $\frac{8 + 9}{2} = 8.5$.

Mode

- The mode is the **most common value**.
- Sometimes there are **several modes**.
- If there are **three or more** numbers that occur equally often, we say there is **no mode**.

Examples:

1 **(7) 11 23 (7) 5 (7) 13 22 14 16 9 17 5**

The most common number is **7**: there are three of them.

The mode of this data set is 7.

2 **(15) 2 (15) 4 5 17 8 (13) 11 (13) 9 12 6**

Both **13** and **15** occur twice.

The modes are 13 and 15.

3 **46 (45) (52) 39 (45) 47 (49) (52) 41 44 (49)**

There are three numbers that occur equally often: **45**, **49** and **52**.

There is no mode.

If there are **three or more** 'modes', we say there is **no mode** at all.

 ISBN: 9780170451833

Calculate the mean, median and mode for these data sets. Round any calculations to 3 sf.

1 0 0 5 8 9 9 14 17 19 19 20 22 24

Mean = ____________ Median = ____________ Mode = ____________

2 0.1 0.4 0.7 0.7 0.8 1.0 1.3 1.6 1.8 2.3 3.2 3.4 3.4 3.9

Mean = ____________ Median = ____________ Mode = ____________

3 0 2 4 4 6 6 7 9 12 13 17 19

Mean = ____________ Median = ____________ Mode = ____________

4

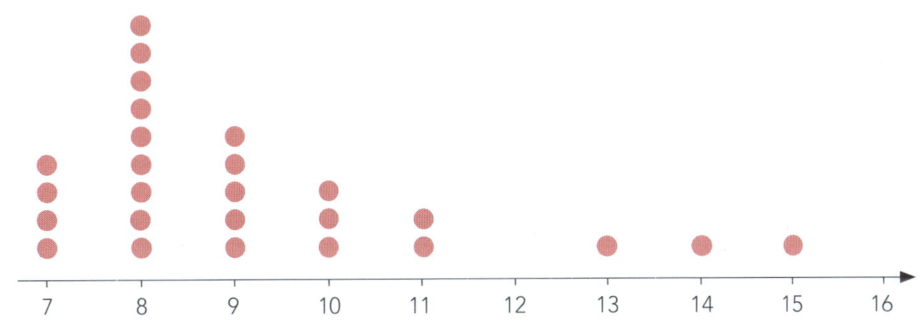

Mean = ____________ Median = ____________ Mode = ____________

5

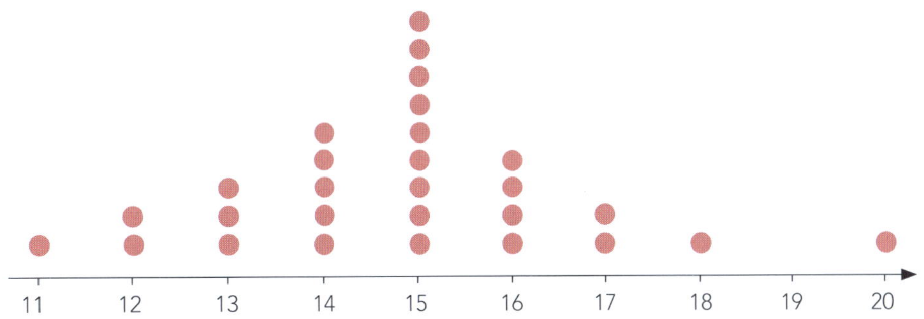

Mean = ____________ Median = ____________ Mode = ____________

ISBN: 9780170451833

Measures of spread

Range

- The range is the **maximum value minus the minimum value** in the data set.
- Note: the range is a **single number**.
- Like the mean, the range is affected by unusually large or small values.
- The data does not need to be in order to calculate the range.
- The range is a measure of the **variability** of the data.

Range = maximum – minimum

Quartiles

- The upper quartile (UQ) is the **median** of the **top half** of the data.
- The lower quartile (LQ) is the **median** of the **bottom half** of the data.
- The quartiles and the median divide the data into quarters.

Interquartile range (IQR) = upper quartile (UQ) – lower quartile (LQ)

Examples:

1 If the number of pieces of data is **odd**, **exclude** the median from the top and bottom halves of the data.

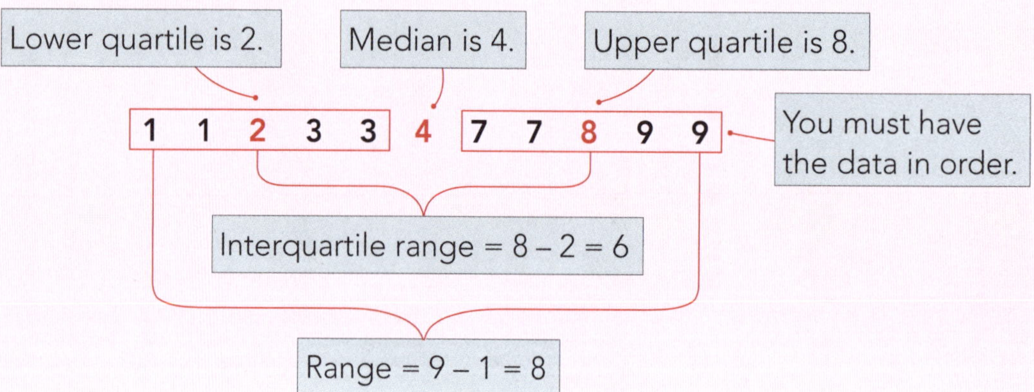

2 If the number of pieces of data is **even**, find the median values of the top and bottom halves of the data.

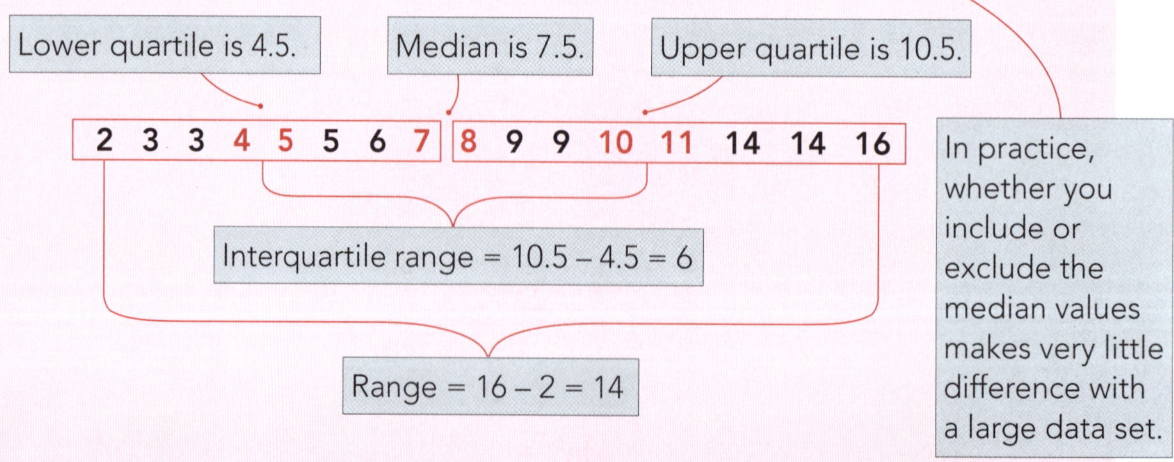

Ranges and interquartile ranges are used to measure the variability of groups of data.

ISBN: 9780170451833

Calculate the statistics for the following data sets.

1 **5 7 12 15 18 23 28 29 30 34 41 46 48 53**

Minimum = _____ LQ = _____ Median = _____ UQ = _____ Maximum = _____

Range = ____________ Interquartile range = ____________

2 **12 14 18 19 24 28 29 31 34 37 40**

Minimum = _____ LQ = _____ Median = _____ UQ = _____ Maximum = _____

Range = ____________ Interquartile range = ____________

3 **2 3 3 4 5 6 7 9 9 10 12 12 15 16 18 20 20**

Minimum = _____ LQ = _____ Median = _____ UQ = _____ Maximum = _____

Range = ____________ Interquartile range = ____________

4

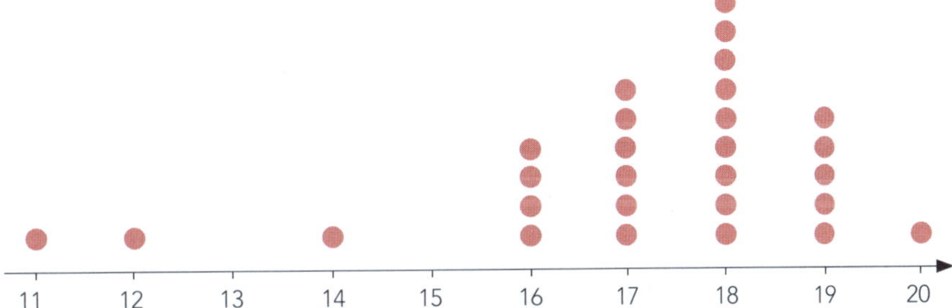

Minimum = _____ LQ = _____ Median = _____ UQ = _____ Maximum = _____

Range = ____________ Interquartile range = ____________

5

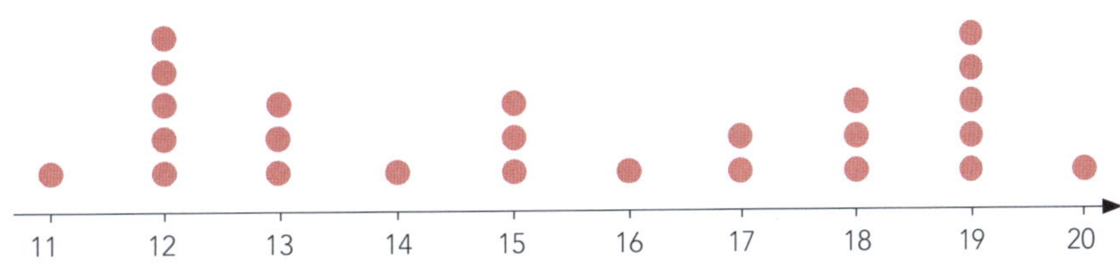

Minimum = _____ LQ = _____ Median = _____ UQ = _____ Maximum = _____

Range = ____________ Interquartile range = ____________

ISBN: 9780170451833

Unusual features

- These could be an **unusual point** or **clusters**.
- An unusual point is one that is away from the rest of the data.
- A cluster is a group of data that is away from the rest of the data.

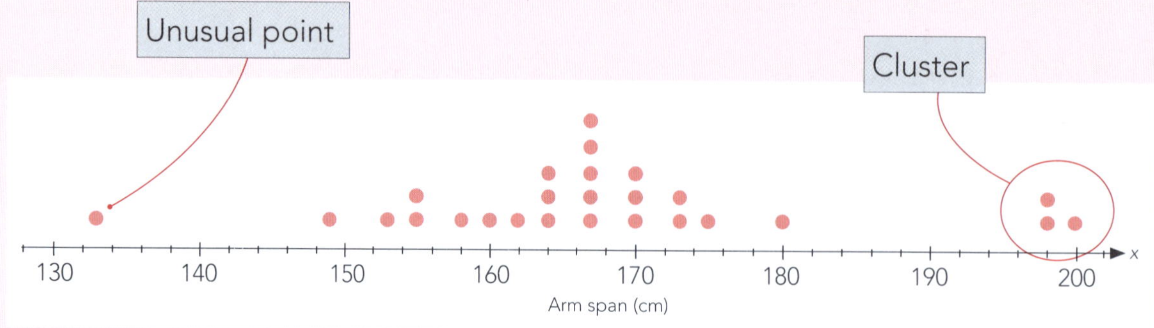

What to do with unusual features?

- If you have collected the data, it pays to check and correct any collection or recording errors.
- If there are no errors, think about whether the unusual feature is possible and state your thoughts in your summary.

How many makes a cluster?

Don't get hung up on labels and definitions. It's best to write what you see. If there are two points away from the rest of the data, then say that!

Effects of unusual points

- The **mean** and the **range** are **affected** by unusual points.
- The **median**, **mode**, **quartiles** and **interquartile range** are **usually unaffected**.

No unusual points ⇒ either the **median or mean** are usually good measures of centre.

Unusual points ⇒ likely that the **median** is a better measure of centre.

Example:

3 33 35 36 37 39 41

Mean $= \frac{224}{7}$ $= 32$ Median = 36 Mode = none Range = 41 – 3 = 38 IQR = 39 – 33 = 6

The median (36) is a better measure of centre than the mean (32) because the mean is smaller than all but one value in the data set.

The IQR (6) is a better measure of spread than the range (38) because the range of the highest six numbers is only 8.

It can be hard to identify unusual points with a list. They are easier to see on a graph.

 ISBN: 9780170451833

Calculate the median and the mean for these data sets and answer the questions.

1 **3 5 6 8 9 9 12 36**

Median = ________ Mean = ________

The mean and the median are similar/different. Explain why. ________________________

____

2 **12 15 16 18 18 19 21 24 27**

Median = ________ Mean = ________

The mean and the median are similar/different. Explain why. ________________________

____

3 **2 34 57 63 72 74 76 81 88 89**

Median = ________ Mean = ________

The mean and the median are similar/different. Explain why. ________________________

____

4

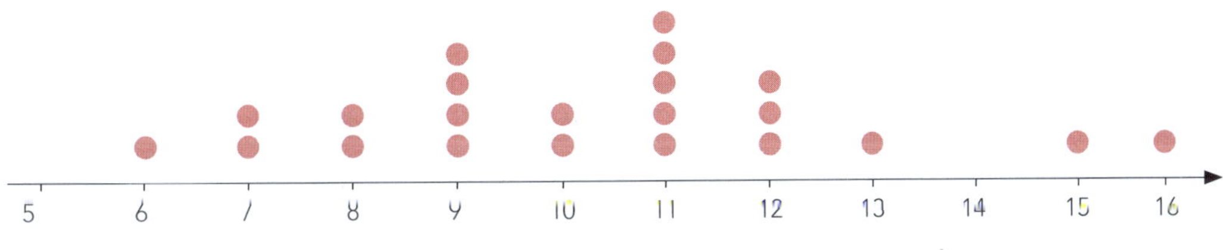

Median = ________ Mean = ________

The mean and the median are similar/different. Explain why. ________________________

____

5

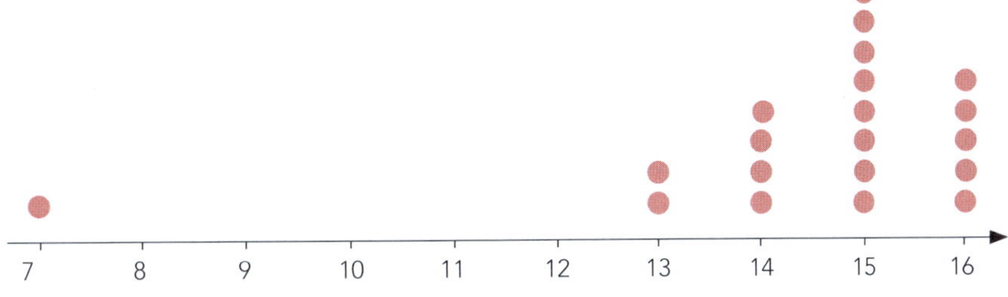

Median = ________ Mean = ________

The mean and the median are similar/different. Explain why. ________________________

____

ISBN: 9780170451833

Box plots

- These are used to display **discrete** or **continuous** data.
- They are very useful for comparing sets of data.
- These are sometimes called '**box and whisker plots**'. The whiskers are the lines between the box and the highest and lowest values.

For a box plot you need the following:

minimum   lower quartile   median   upper quartile   maximum

Example:

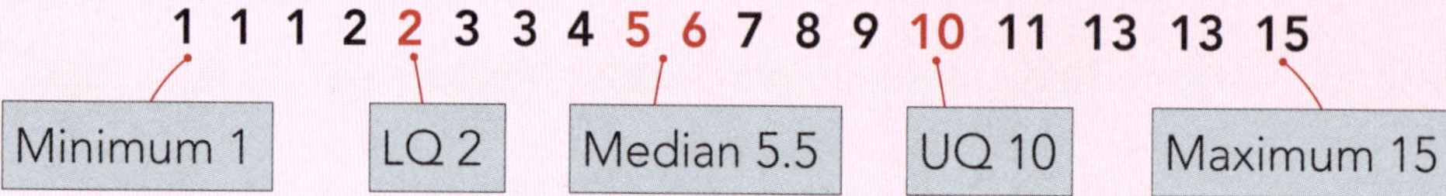

These 5 points divide the data into quarters.

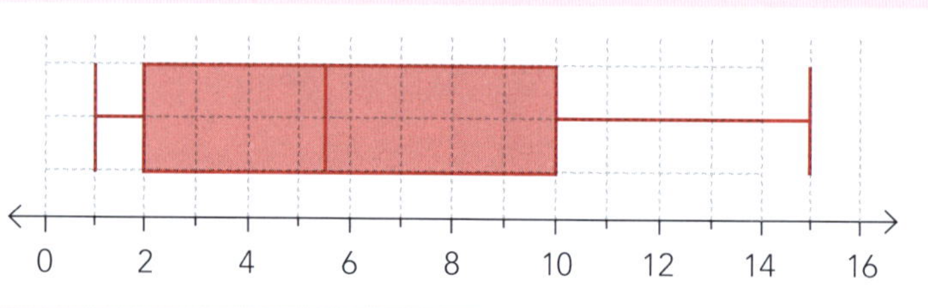

Answer the following questions.

1 Complete this diagram by using the words in the box.

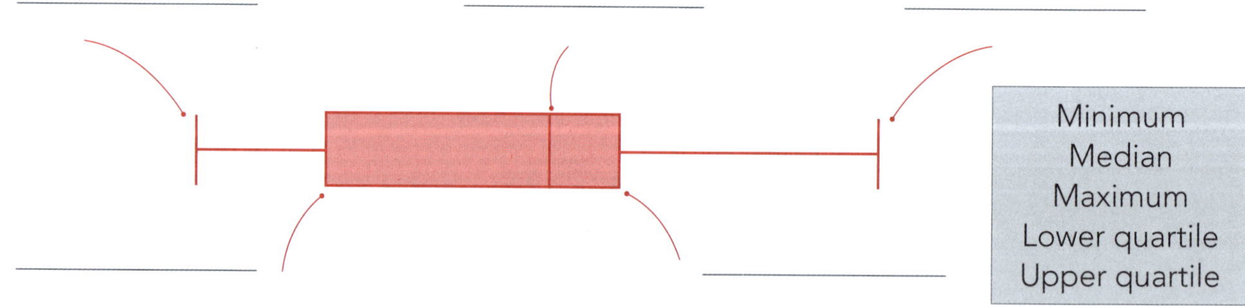

2 Draw a box plot for these statistics.

Minimum = 1   LQ = 5   Median = 13   UQ = 17   Maximum = 20

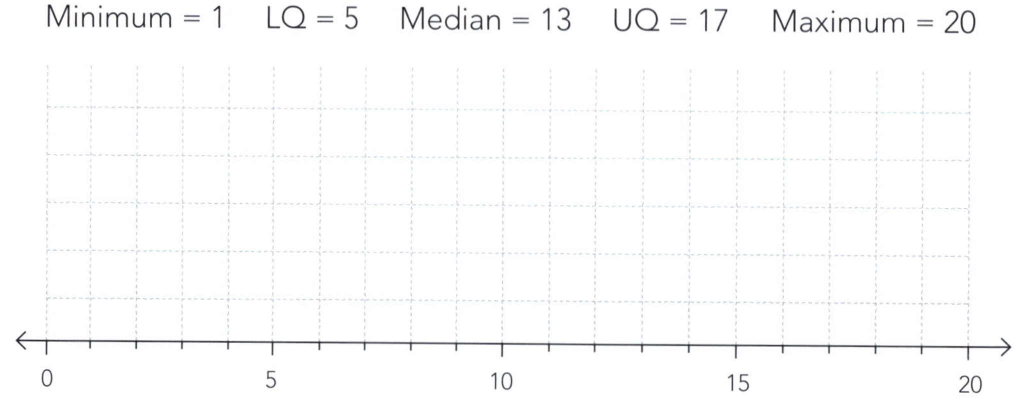

ISBN: 9780170451833

Calculate the required statistics and then draw box plots for the following.

3 **1 2 2 4 10 11 12 12 13 14 14 14 15 15 19 20**

Minimum = ______ LQ = ______ Median = ______ UQ = ______ Maximum = ______

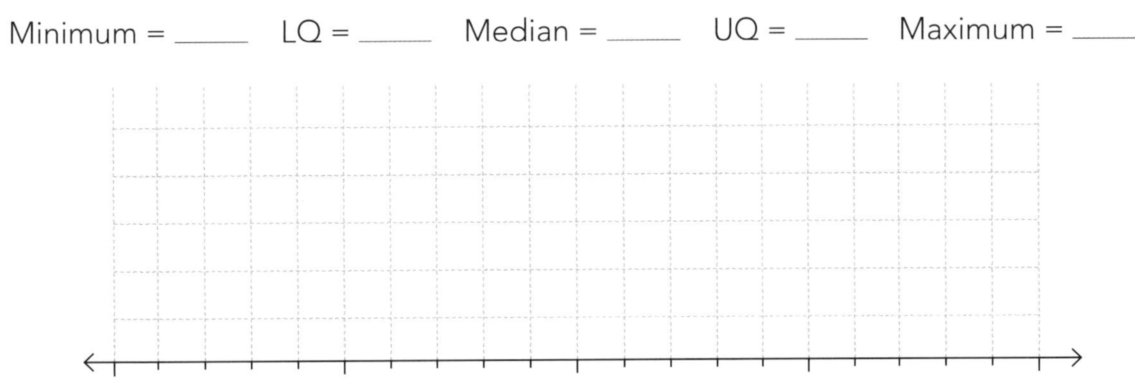

4 **0 0 2 3 4 4 4 6 6 7 15 16 18 20 20**

Minimum = ______ LQ = ______ Median = ______ UQ = ______ Maximum = ______

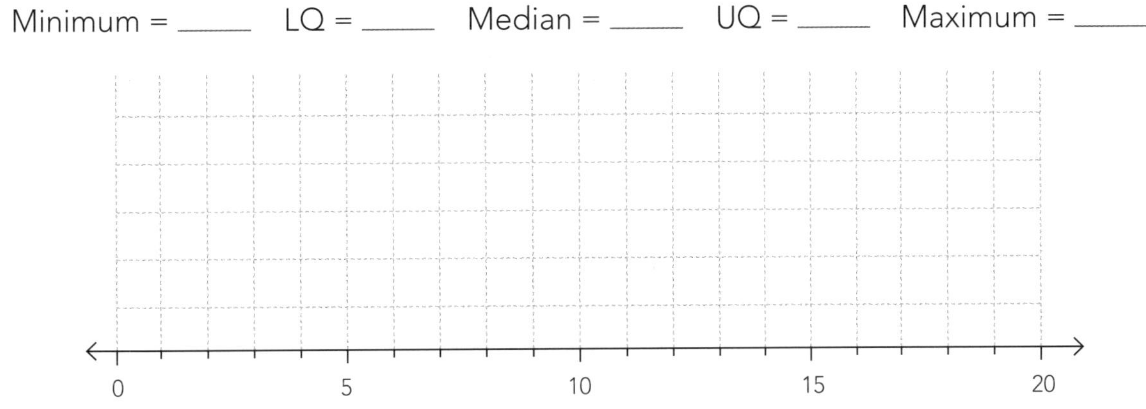

5 **0.5 1 4 5 5.5 5.5 6.5 6.5 9.5 9.5 9.5 10**

____

Minimum = ______ LQ = ______ Median = ______ UQ = ______ Maximum = ______

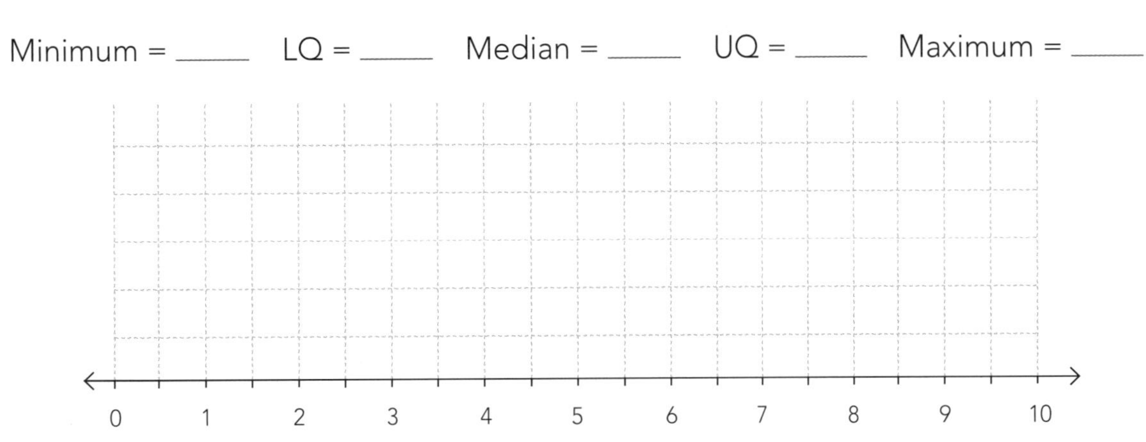

ISBN: 9780170451833

Understanding box plots

You need to understand the meanings of different parts of a box plot.

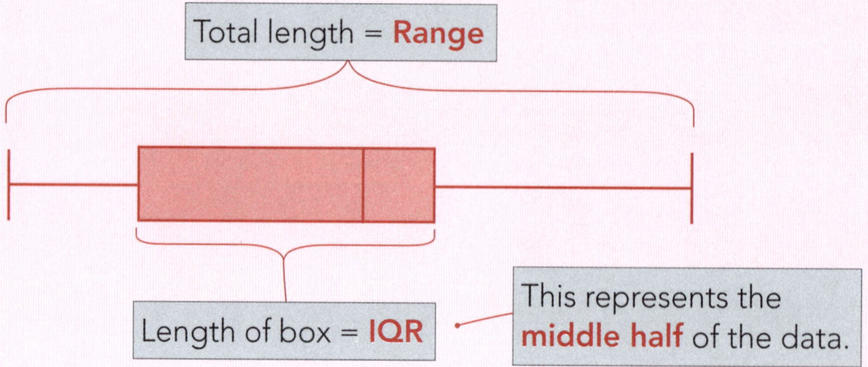

Data is symmetrically distributed ⇒ box plot will be symmetrical.

Data is not symmetrically distributed ⇒ box plot will not be symmetrical.

Example:

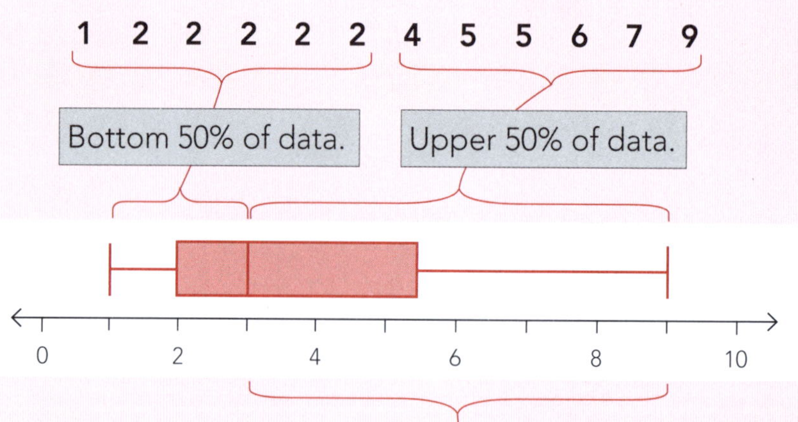

The upper 50% of the box plot looks longer because the data is **more spread out**. It does **not** contain more data.

The **vertical lines** on a box plot divide the data into **quarters**.

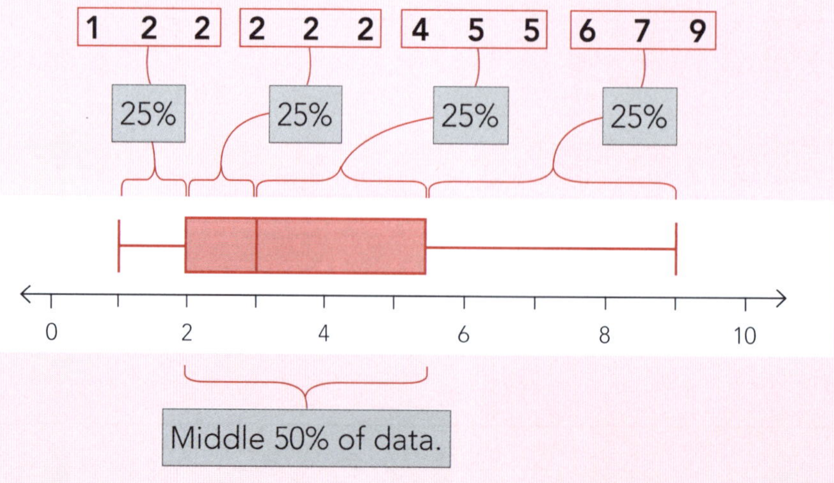

ISBN: 9780170451833

Fill in the missing percentages and terms below.

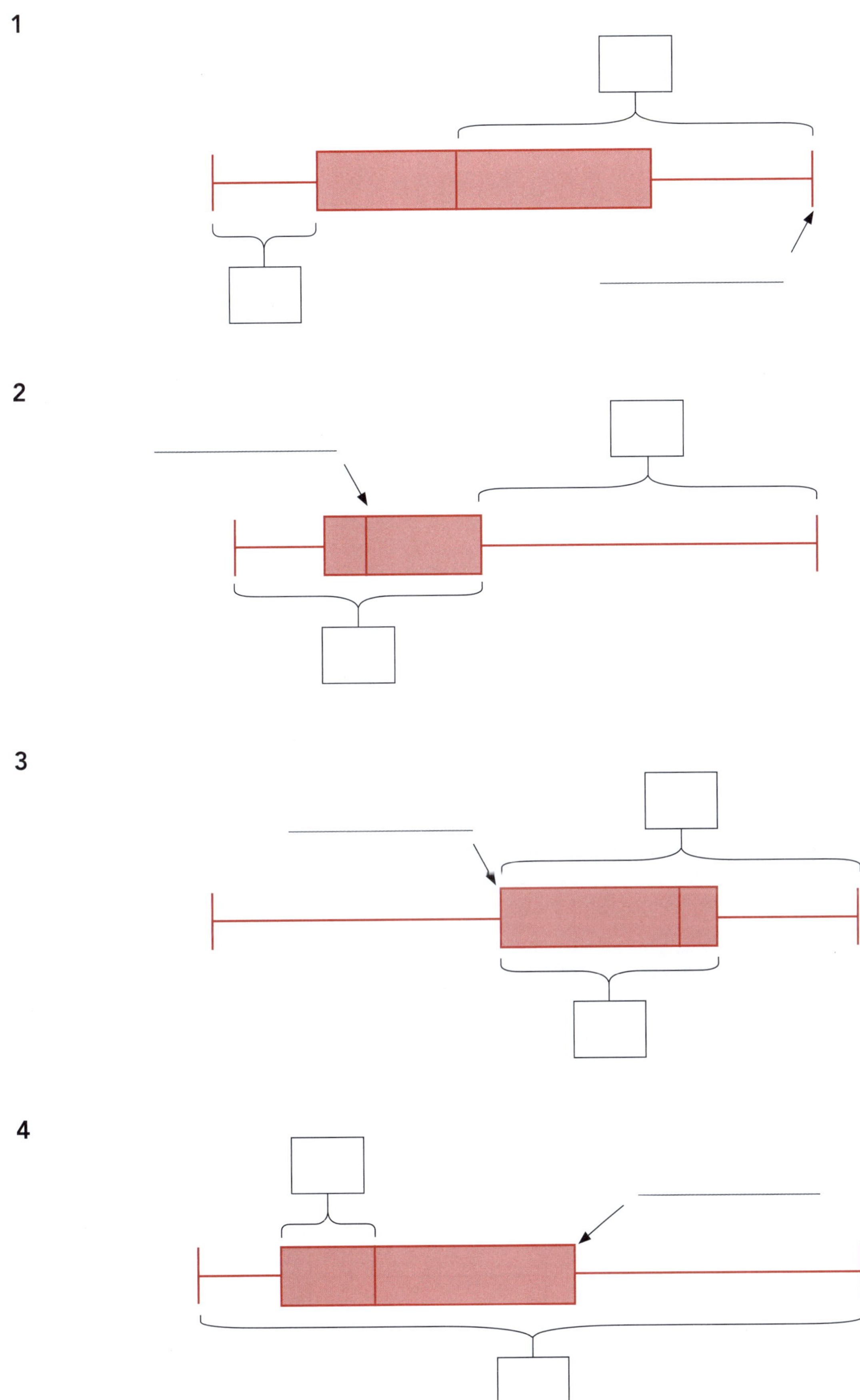

ISBN: 9780170451833

Comparing box plots

Box plots are a useful way of comparing several groups of data.

Example:

A

B

The median of B is larger than the median of A. ✓
The interquartile range of B is larger than that of A. ✗
The median of A is lower than the lower quartile of B. ✓
The ranges of A and B are about the same. ✓

Identify if these statements are correct or incorrect.

1 Arm span of students

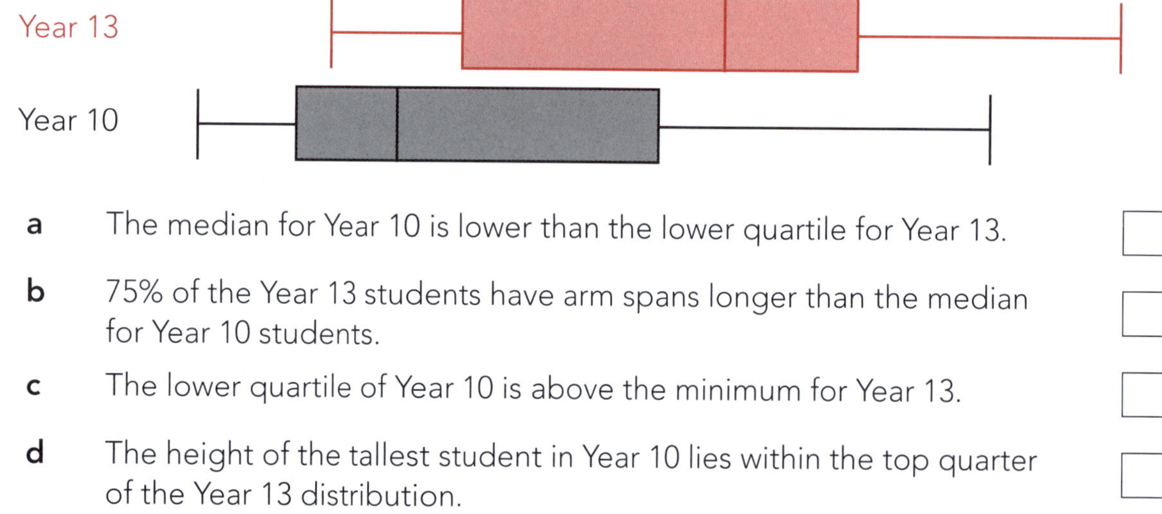

a The median for Year 10 is lower than the lower quartile for Year 13. ☐

b 75% of the Year 13 students have arm spans longer than the median for Year 10 students. ☐

c The lower quartile of Year 10 is above the minimum for Year 13. ☐

d The height of the tallest student in Year 10 lies within the top quarter of the Year 13 distribution. ☐

2 Heights of Year 9 and 10 boys

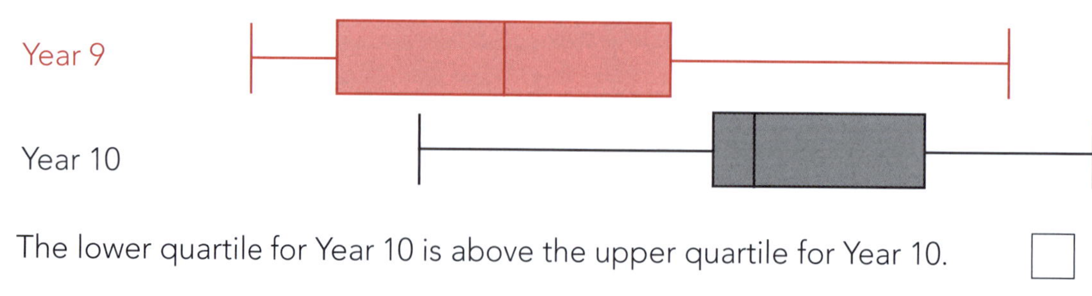

a The lower quartile for Year 10 is above the upper quartile for Year 10. ☐

b 75% of Year 9 boys are shorter than 75% of Year 10 boys. ☐

c The median of Year 9 is lower than the minimum of Year 10. ☐

ISBN: 9780170451833

Interpret the graphs and answer these statements about students' heights.

3

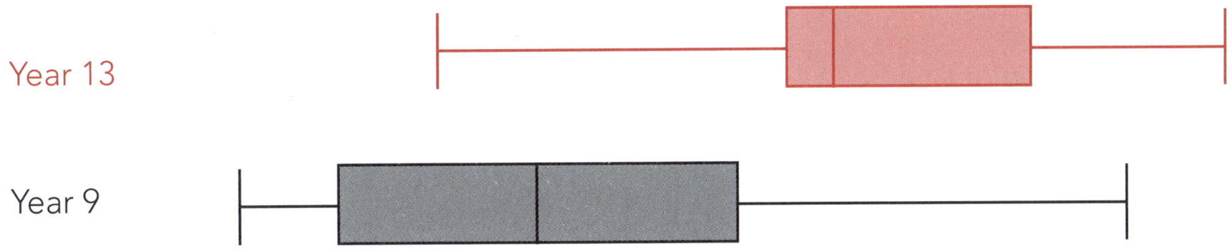

Year 13

Year 9

a 'Year 13 students are taller than the Year 9 students.'

☐ Agree ☐ Disagree ☐ Can't tell for sure

Explain your answer. ____

____

b 'At least one Year 9 student is taller than 75% of Year 13 students.'

☐ Agree ☐ Disagree ☐ Can't tell for sure

Explain your answer. ____

____

4

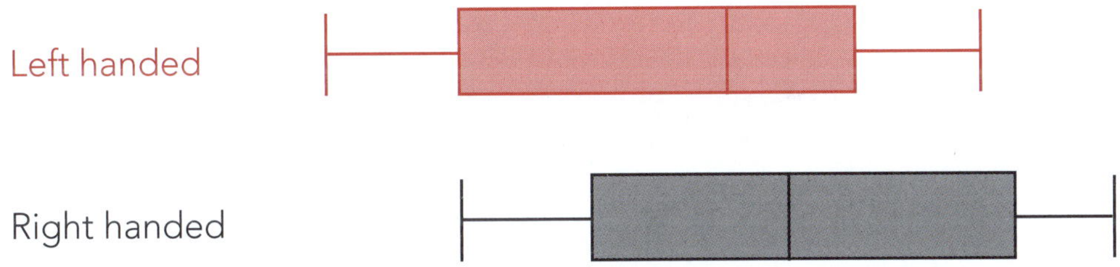

Left handed

Right handed

a 'Right-handed students are taller than left-handed students.'

☐ Agree ☐ Disagree ☐ Can't tell for sure

Explain your answer. ____

____

b 'There are no students who are unusually tall.'

☐ Agree ☐ Disagree ☐ Can't tell for sure

Explain your answer. ____

____

ISBN: 9780170451833

Challenge 2

Match each dot plot to a box plot below.

1

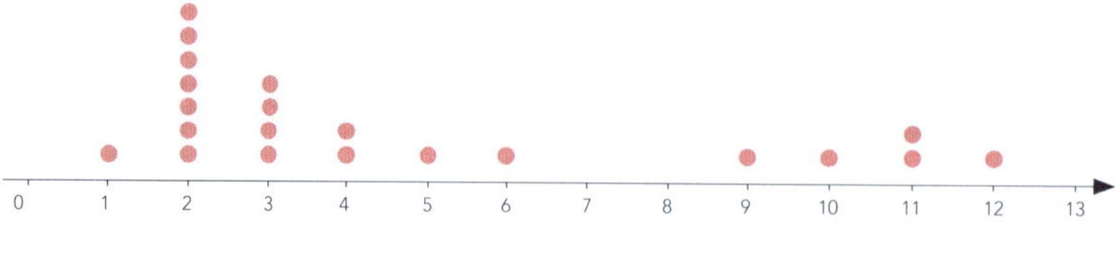

2

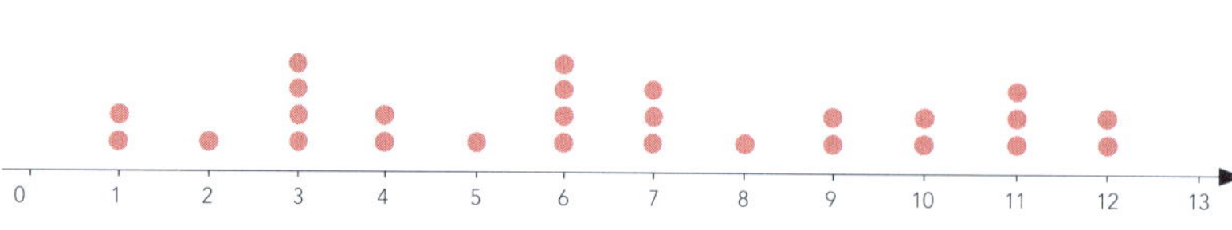

3

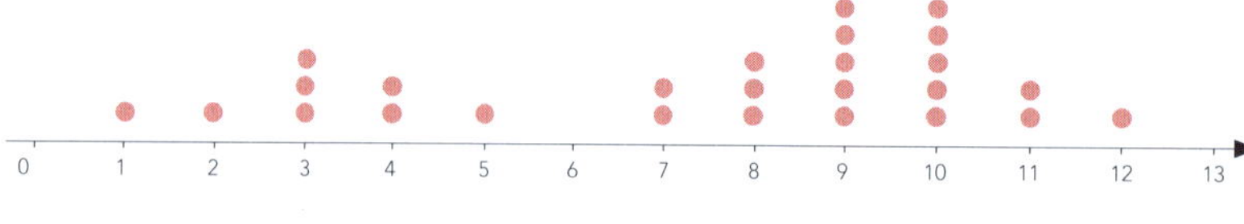

A

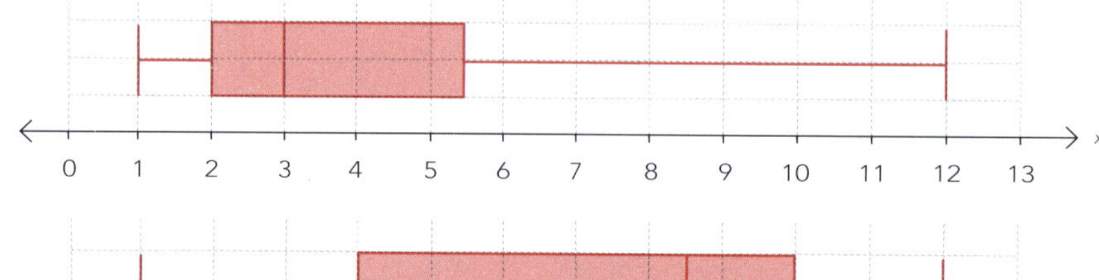

B

C

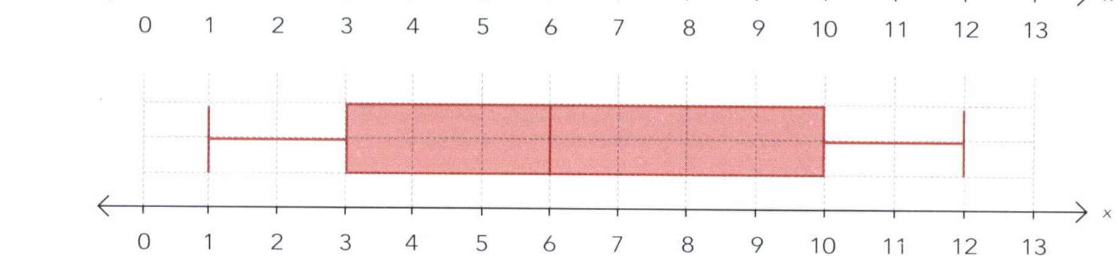

Thinking about dot and box plots.

4 What does a dot plot show us that a box plot doesn't?

5 What does a box plot show us that a dot plot doesn't?

6 What do both show?

ISBN: 9780170451833

Challenge 3

1 If a very low value were removed from a large data set:

		✓, maybe or ✗
a	the mean will increase.	
b	the median will increase.	
c	the IQR will stay the same.	
d	the range will stay the same.	

2 Match the sets of data to the box plots.

a  ______

b  ______

c 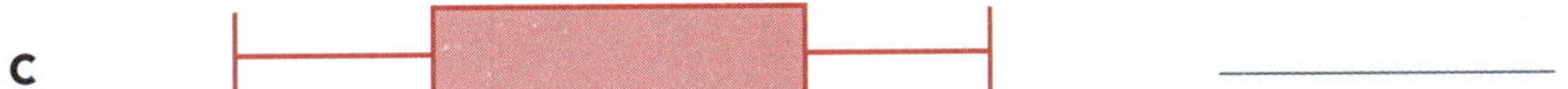 ______

d 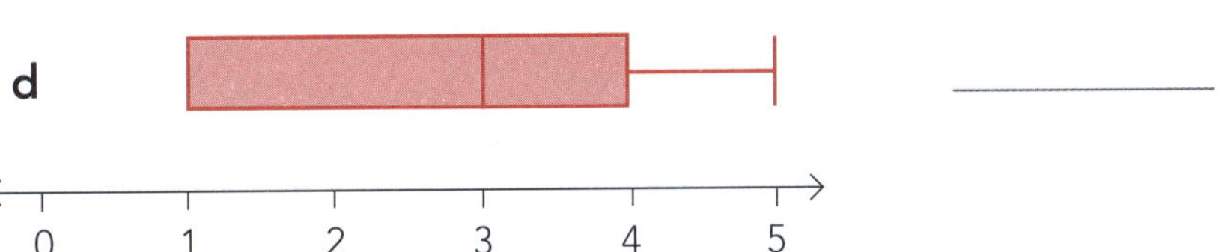 ______

1	1 1 1 2 3 3 4 4 5	2	1 1 2 3 4 4 4 5 5
3	1 1 2 2 2 3 3 4 5	4	1 1 2 2 3 4 5 5 5

3 Without calculating the median or mean, decide which would have similar means and medians.

		Similar	Different
a			
b			
c			

Revision 1

Round any calculations to 3 sf.

1 Convert these probabilities into decimals and state which is more likely.

$\frac{2}{9}$ = ________ $\frac{7}{35}$ = ________ More likely: ________

2 'How tall are you?' is an example of a ______________ question, and the answer will produce ______________ data.

3 Jay walks to school 65% of the time and the rest of the time he gets a ride. If Jay gets a ride, the likelihood of him making his lunch is 0.84. If Jay walks to school, there is a 1 in 5 chance that he will make his lunch.

a Complete the tree diagram.

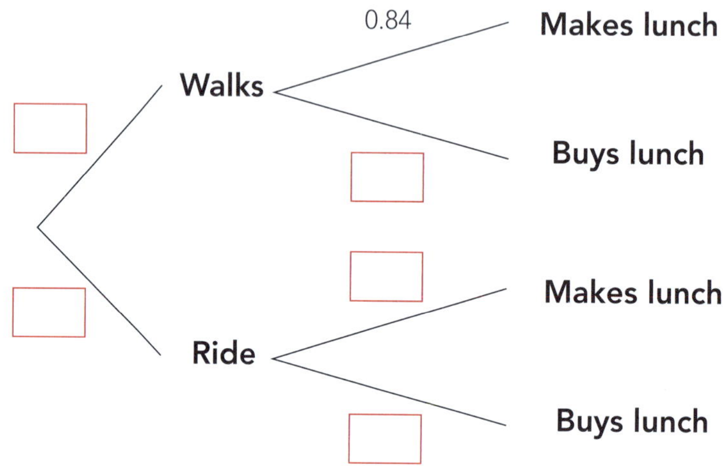

b Calculate the probability that Jay gets a ride and buys his lunch. __________

c Calculate the probability that Jay makes his lunch. __________

4 What is the most popular phone brand in the North Island?

To find the answer, NZ should: ☐ do a census ☐ take a sample

5 **a** The three types of variables are continuous, descriptive and

______________________.

b Give an example of a descriptive variable. ______________________

c The distance to the closest shop is a ______________________ variable.

6 Pie graphs are used to display ______________________ data.

 ISBN: 9780170451833

7 The New Zealand police collect the demographics of victims of motor vehicle theft. The graph shows the ages and sexes of victims of motor vehicle theft during 2021.

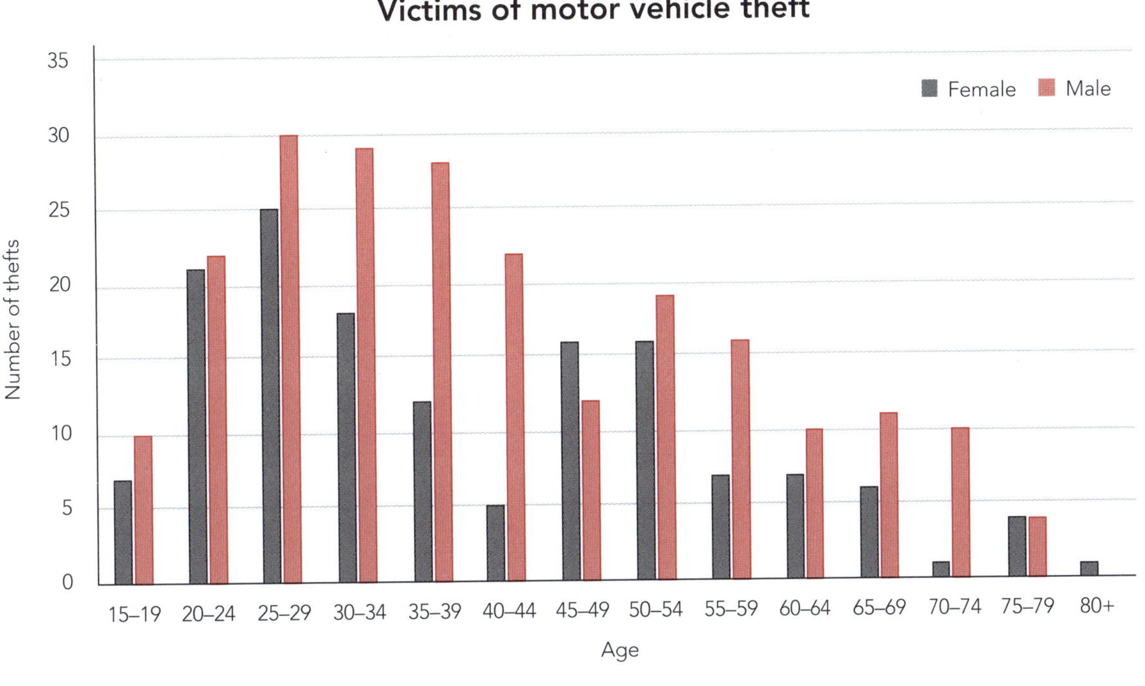

a Which age group were the most likely victims? ______________

b How many victims were females aged between 40 and 44? ______________

c Which year group saw an equal number of female and male victims? ______________

d 'Males are more likely to be a victim of car theft than females.'

☐ Agree ☐ Disagree ☐ Can't tell for sure

Explain your answer. ____

____

e 'Thieves don't like to steal vehicles owned by old people.'

☐ Agree ☐ Disagree ☐ Can't tell for sure

Explain your answer. ____

____

ISBN: 9780170451833

8 Arm span of Year 10 and 12 students.

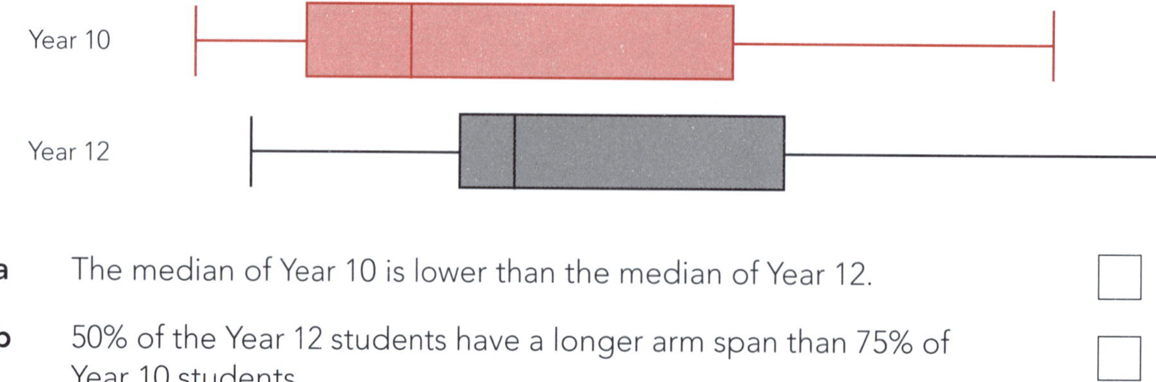

a The median of Year 10 is lower than the median of Year 12. ☐

b 50% of the Year 12 students have a longer arm span than 75% of Year 10 students. ☐

c Half of the Year 10 students have a shorter arm span than more than 75% of the Year 12 students. ☐

9 The Ministry of Education information about permanent school leavers in 2018.

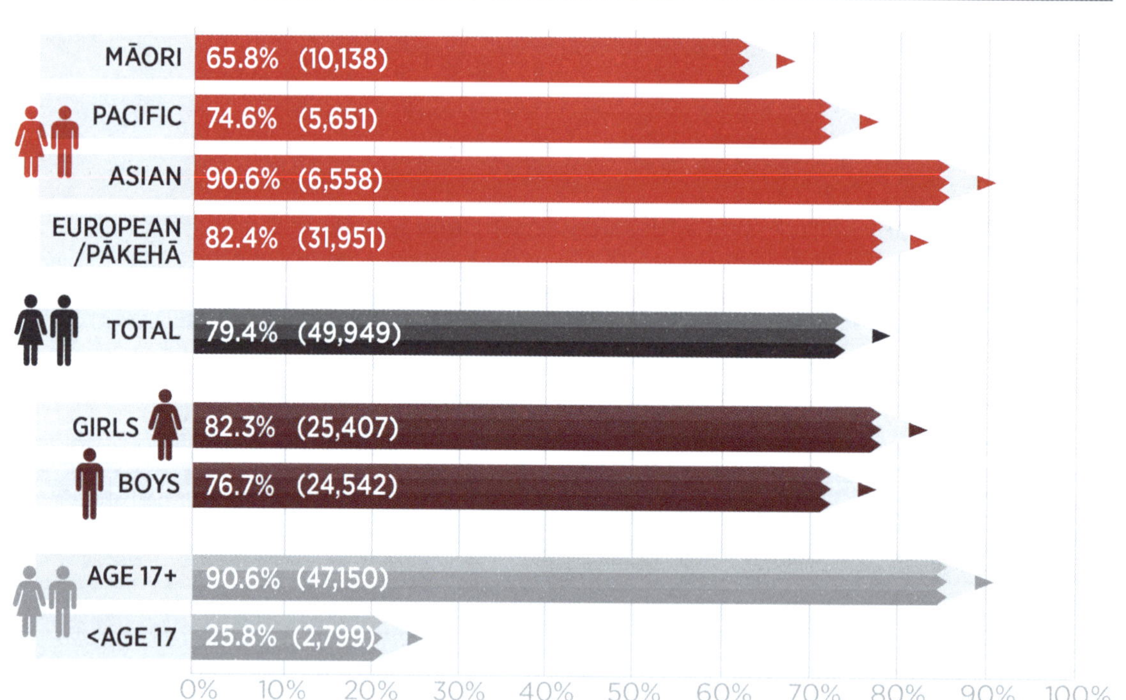

a Which ethnicity is most likely to leave school with NCEA Level 2 or above? __________

b What percentage of students in 2018 left without NCEA Level 2 or above? __________

c If a permanent school leaver with NCEA Level 2 or above in 2018 was selected at random, what is the probability that they are under 17 years old? __________

 ISBN: 9780170451833

Revision 2

Round any calculations to 3 sf.

1 Convert these probabilities into decimals and state which is more likely.

36 in 95: ________ $\frac{19}{50}$ = ________ More likely: ________

2 'How many Year 13 boys and how many Year 13 girls have driver licences?' is an example of a ______________ question, and the answer will produce ______________ data.

3 Students select one of the subjects below.

	Food technology	**Digital technology**	**Mechanics**	**Totals**
Year 9		36		
Year 10	57		29	125
Totals			**74**	**268**

a Complete the table.

b What is the probability that a student selects Food technology? ________

c What proportion of students are in Year 9? ________

d What is the probability that a student is in Year 9 and does Mechanics?

____

e What percentage of Year 10 students do Digital technology? ________

4 Should New Zealand change the voting age to 16?

To find the answer, NZ should: ☐ do a census ☐ take a sample

5 **a** The three types of variables are discrete, continuous and

______________.

b Give an example of a discrete variable. ______________

c The brand of shampoo in your shower is a ______________ variable.

6 What type of data can be used in a bar graph? ______________

7 'Did you have a bath this morning?' is an example of an open/a closed question.

ISBN: 9780170451833

8 Babies born in New Zealand with the names Cooper, Hugo and Braxton.

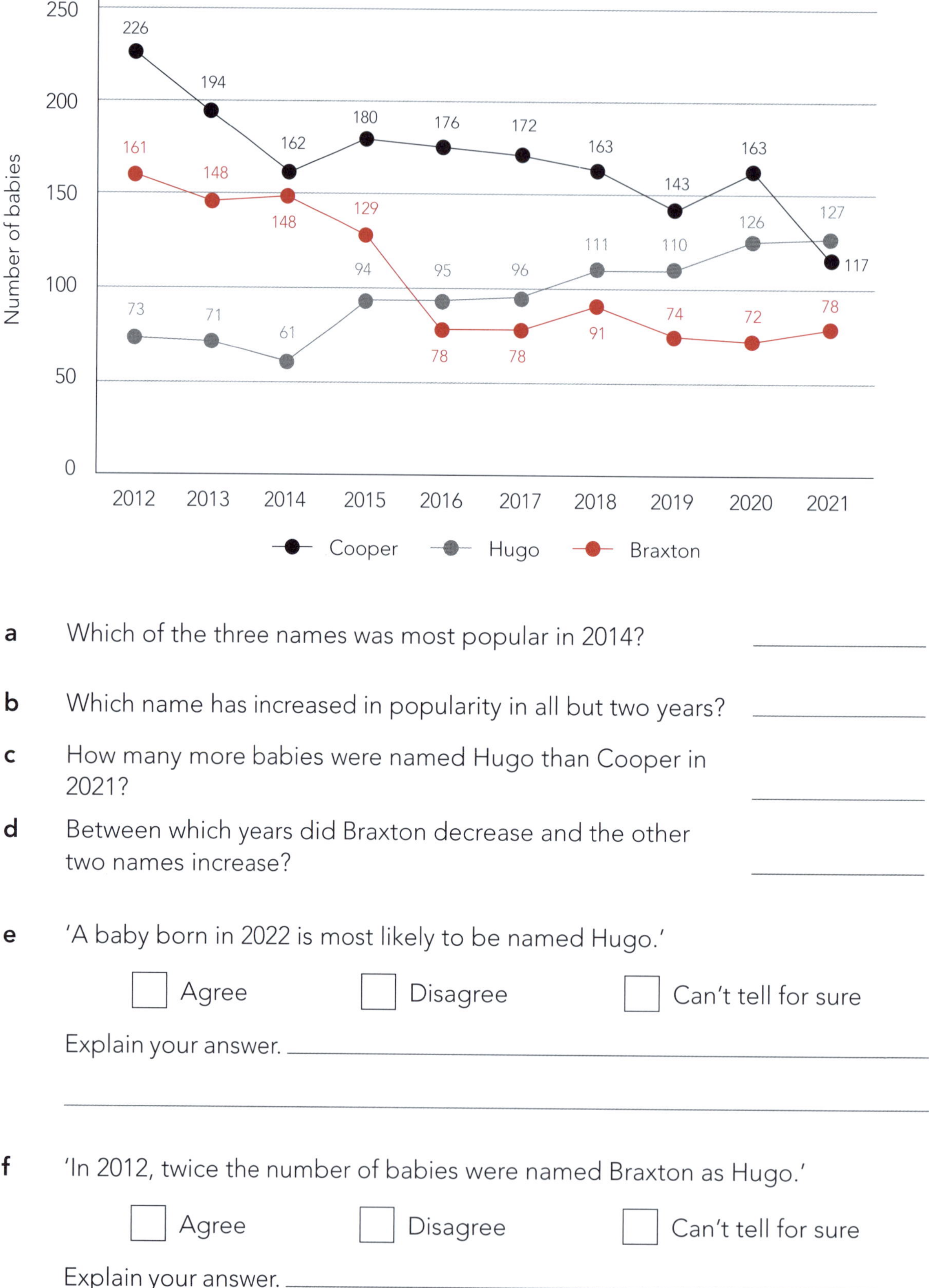

a Which of the three names was most popular in 2014? __________

b Which name has increased in popularity in all but two years? __________

c How many more babies were named Hugo than Cooper in 2021? __________

d Between which years did Braxton decrease and the other two names increase? __________

e 'A baby born in 2022 is most likely to be named Hugo.'

☐ Agree ☐ Disagree ☐ Can't tell for sure

Explain your answer. __________

f 'In 2012, twice the number of babies were named Braxton as Hugo.'

☐ Agree ☐ Disagree ☐ Can't tell for sure

Explain your answer. __________

ISBN: 9780170451833

9 Records of temperature and ice cream sales were collected for a week. Are the following statements true or false?

a Monday was hotter than Wednesday. True/False

b More ice creams were sold on Sunday than on Saturday. True/False

c Saturday was cooler than Friday, but more ice creams were sold. True/False

d Wednesday was warmer than Sunday, but fewer ice creams were sold. True/False

10 The graph shows the age distribution of New Zealand teachers.

Teacher age group

Ages	<25	25–34	35–44	45–54	55–64	65–74	75+
Number of teachers	3% (2,062)	19% (13,328)	23% (16,303)	25% (17,835)	20% (14,465)	10% (6,958)	1% (637)

Number of teachers axis: 0, 5,000, 10,000, 15,000, 20,000

a Which age range are most teachers in? ________________

b 'Most teachers are old.'

☐ Agree ☐ Disagree ☐ Can't tell for sure

Explain your answer. ____

____

ISBN: 9780170451833

Answers

Probability (pp. 6–19)

Fraction, decimal and percentage revision (p. 6)

Fraction	Decimal	Percentage	Probability in words
$\frac{17}{20}$	0.85	85%	Unlikely
$\frac{1}{20}$	0.05	5%	Very unlikely
$\frac{27}{80}$	0.3375	33.75%	Unlikely
$\frac{3}{500}$	0.006	0.6%	Extremely unlikely
$\frac{1}{100}$	0.01	1%	Very likely
$\frac{1}{200}$	0.005	0.5%	Extremely unlikely
$\frac{195}{200}$	0.975	97.5%	Extremely likely

Probability revision (pp. 7–8)

1 1 in 16 = 0.0625

2 So the probability of tossing a coin and getting four heads is slightly more likely.
1 in 7776 = 0.0001 (1 sf)
So the probability of throwing a die five times and getting five heads is more likely.

Expected number (p. 9)

1 a 25 times b 50 times

2 5 answers

3 192 or 193 students (not 192.7)

4 400 000 people 5 7000 plants

6 12 500

Ways of calculating probabilities (p. 10)

1 Theoretical 2 Experimental

3 Experimental 4 Theoretical

5 Theoretical

Tree diagrams (pp. 11–16)

1 a

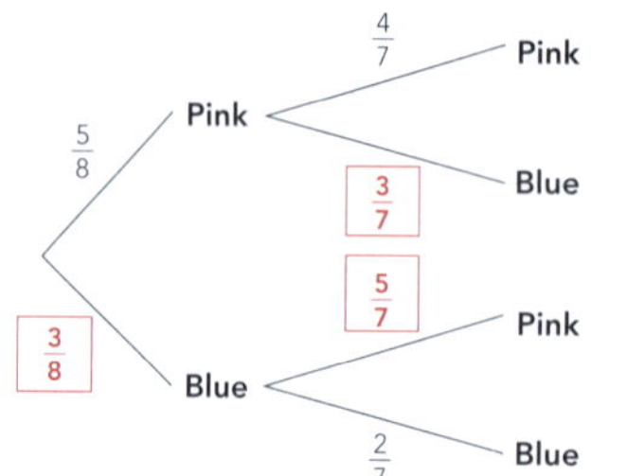

$P(PP) = \frac{5}{8} \times \frac{4}{7} = \frac{20}{56} = 0.357$

$P(PB) = \frac{5}{8} \times \frac{3}{7} = \frac{15}{56} = 0.268$

$P(BP) = \frac{3}{8} \times \frac{5}{7} = \frac{15}{56} = 0.268$

$P(BB) = \frac{3}{8} \times \frac{2}{7} = \frac{6}{56} = 0.107$

b 0.107 c 0.536

d 0.357 e 0.893

f 18 times

2 a

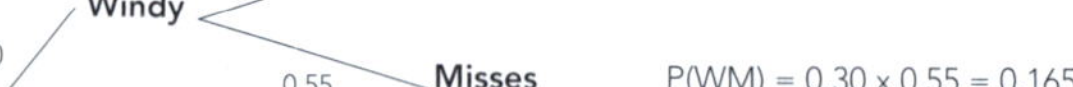

0.45, Windy, 0.30, Gets it

b 0.135 c 0.354

d 0.811 e 0.865

f 5 or 6

3 a

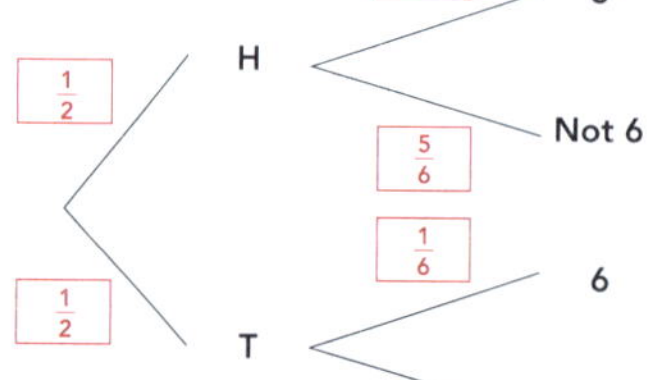

$P(H6) = \frac{1}{2} \times \frac{1}{6} = \frac{1}{12} = 0.08\dot{3}$

$P(H6') = \frac{1}{2} \times \frac{5}{6} = \frac{5}{12} = 0.41\dot{6}$

$P(T6) = \frac{1}{2} \times \frac{1}{6} = \frac{1}{12} = 0.08\dot{3}$

$P(T6') = \frac{1}{2} \times \frac{5}{6} = \frac{5}{12} = 0.41\dot{6}$

b $0.08\dot{3}$ c $0.83\dot{3}$

d $0.58\dot{3}$ e 0.5

f 8 (not 8.33) g 4 (not 4.17)

4

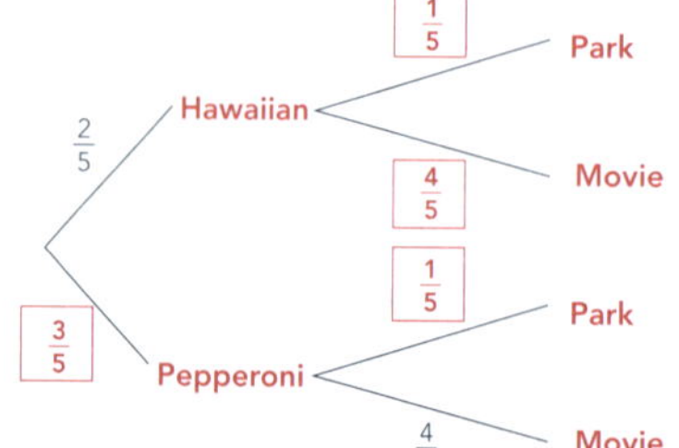

$P(HP) = \frac{2}{5} \times \frac{1}{5} = \frac{2}{25} = 0.08$

$P(HM) = \frac{2}{5} \times \frac{4}{5} = \frac{8}{25} = 0.32$

$P(PP) = \frac{3}{5} \times \frac{1}{5} = \frac{3}{25} = 0.12$

$P(PM) = \frac{3}{5} \times \frac{4}{5} = \frac{12}{25} = 0.48$

 ISBN: 9780170451833

5 a

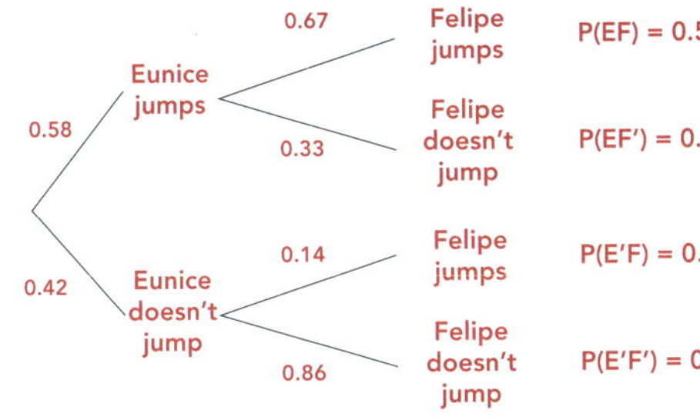

b 0.389　　c 0.361
d 0.250

Probabilities from tables (pp. 17–19)

1 a 0.043 or $\frac{7}{164}$　　b 0.646 or $\frac{106}{164}$

c 0.338 or $\frac{53}{159}$　　d 28.6%

2 a

	Been skiing	Never been skiing	Totals
Australian	82	215	297
New Zealander	208	64	272
Totals	290	279	569

b 0.490 or $\frac{279}{569}$　　c 52.2%

d 11.2%　　e 0.724 or $\frac{215}{297}$

f 1.18 million

3 a

	Can juggle	Can't juggle	Totals
Left handed	35	58	93
Right handed	186	245	431
Totals	221	303	524

b 0.578 or $\frac{303}{524}$　　c 17.7%

d 35.5%　　e About 89 400 people

4 a

	Both parents can	One parent can	Neither parent can	Totals
Child can	79	68	22	169
Child cannot	12	23	44	79
Totals	91	91	66	248

b 0.319 or $\frac{79}{248}$　　c 36.7%

d 8.87%　　e 0.402 or $\frac{68}{169}$

5 a

	First class	Second class	Third class	Crew	Totals
Survived	204	118	177	212	711
Died	121	167	529	673	1490
Totals	325	285	706	885	2201

b 58.6%　　c $\frac{285}{1316} = 21.7\%$

d $\frac{817}{1316} = 62.1\%$

Statistical concepts (pp. 20–23)

Census and sample (p. 20)

	Census or sample	Why?
1	Census	The flag is an important issue for New Zealanders.
2	Sample	Toothpaste flavour is not a major issue, and it would be too expensive for a company to do a census.
3	Sample	Ice cream brand is not a major issue, and it would be too expensive for a company to do a census.

Types of variables (p. 21)

1 Descriptive　　2 Discrete
3 Continuous　　4 Descriptive
5 Continuous　　6 Discrete
7 D, E　　8 B, C
9 A

Investigative questions (p. 22)

1 Comparative　　2 Summary
3 Comparative　　4 Relationship
5 Comparative　　6 Summary
7 Relationship　　8 Comparative
9 Relationship

Types of survey questions (p. 23)

1 Closed, binary
2 Closed, multi-choice
3 Open, long or short
4 Open, short
5 Open, long or short

Data display (pp. 24–66)

1 Scatter graph
Discrete or continuous

2 **Pie graph**
Descriptive

3 Tally chart
Descriptive or discrete

4 Dot plot
Discrete descriptive or rounded continuous

5 Box plot
Discrete or continuous

6 Bar graph
Descriptive and discrete

7 Line graph/time series
Discrete and continuous

8 Pictograph
Descriptive or discrete

9 Histogram
Continuous

ISBN: 9780170451833　

Pie graphs (pp. 26–29)

1 a Where did your injury or fall occur?
 b Summary c 12%
 d 402 000 e At work
 f 0.418
 g Agree
 Injuries at home and in the community are 39% and falls are 28%, making 67% in total.

2 a 15% b 54%
 c 12.4% d Histogram
 e About 1 150 000 f 0.03 x 0.52 = 0.0156

3 a US$44.4 billion b US$30.1 billion
 c 39.5%
 d True
 Dry and wet food make up 80%. Wet food is 16%, and 16% of 80% = 20%.
 e False
 Dog treat market = 20% of US$69.3 = US$13.86
 Cat treat market = 9% of US$43.1 = US$3.88, so it's actually worth over three and a half times the cat food market.
 f NZ$261 million x 0.64 = US$167.0 million
 167.0 million/112.4 billion = 1.49%

Bar graphs (pp. 30–38)

1 a What are the differences between New Zealand adults and New Zealand Māori with regard to speaking and reading Te Reo Māori?
 b Comparative
 c 18%
 d 25%
 e Can't tell for sure
 The survey did not include children, and more Te Reo Māori is being taught in schools, so it is likely that the percentage that can neither speak nor read it is lower than this.

2 a 2020
 b Touch rugby
 c Covid-19 meant fewer people played sport in 2020.
 d Either: Agree
 In each year, rugby union has had at least 4500 injuries, which is more than any other sport, and it is a very popular sport, which means that this is probably true.
 Or: Can't tell for sure
 We do not know the total number of people that play each sport. To be certain we would need to know the proportion of participants who are injured.
 e Can't tell for sure
 The numbers playing touch rugby may have dropped, in which case the proportion of participants who are injured might have increased.

3 a 4830
 b 16.4%
 c 24.3%
 d Disagree
 There were 144 343 European/Pākehā students and that is 49.2% of all students which is just under half.
 e Disagree
 The numbers of international students increases between Year 9 and Year 13. Also, these figures are for numbers of students in each level within one year. We are not given information on changes in year groups from year to year.

4 a 85%
 b Asian
 c 85, 86 or 87%
 d Agree
 For all decile schools, over 70% left with NCEA Level 1.
 e Disagree
 While a higher percentage of Pacific students have NCEA Level 1, there will be a lot more of European/Pākehā than Pacific students, so the statement is not true.

5 a $0.910 billion
 b Department, variety and misc
 c Homewares and electronics
 d Agree
 A 2% difference in spending is insignificant.
 or
 Can't tell for sure
 We are given percentages of the amount spent on eCommerce. If the total amount of spending on eCommerce increase significantly between 2019 and 2020, then it may have changed substantially.
 e Can't tell for sure
 We have only two years' worth of data.

6 a Television
 b 25%
 c 61%
 d Neon because just 0.45% (5% of 9%) of homes allow tamariki to access to it.
 e Can't tell for sure
 We are given no information about when tamariki have access to the device or platform/service. We know only that in 59% of homes which have a tablet, the tamariki have access to it.

ISBN: 9780170451833

Challenge 1 (p. 39)

- **a** 26–28
- **b** About 0.4 per 100 000
- **c** 2014–15 and 2016–17
- **d** 2013–14
- **e** Agree
  In every year, the drowning rate (people per 100 000) is significantly higher in New Zealand.
- **f** Disagree
  The drowning rate per 100 000 of population is given.

Line graphs (pp. 40–43)

1
- **a** How does the unemployment rate for males differ from that for females between 2018 and 2021?
- **b** Comparative
- **c** 4.8%
- **d** 0.3%
- **e** Q3 and Q4 2018
- **f** Q3 2021
- **g** Agree
  Agree assuming the numbers of adult females and males are approximately the same. In all quarters except one, the unemployment rate was greater for females.
- **h** Can't tell for sure
  We are given no information about how much females and males are paid.

2
- **a** $80 or $90 million
- **b** April or May
- **c** Alert Level 3
- **d** January
- **e** It is after Christmas, when New Zealanders spend a lot, and during a time when many go on holiday.
- **f** Disagree
  The graph makes it look as though three times as much was spent, because the *y*-axis doesn't start at 0. In fact, very close to twice as much was spent.

3
- **a** 51%
- **b** 9.00 p.m.
- **c** 52%
- **d** Histogram
- **e** Agree
  51% are still allowed access at 9.00 p.m.
- **f** Disagree
  3% are still allowed access at 10 p.m., so 97% have been stopped by 10 p.m.

Histograms (pp. 44–46)

1
- **a** 2133
- **b** 0.129

2
- **a** What were the ages of the people who made ACC claims for e-scooter related injuries?
- **b** Summative
- **c** 20 to 30 year olds
- **d** 50.2%
- **e** 709 and 564
- **f** $2410.00 (3 sf)
- **g** Can't tell for sure
  There is no data on how many people used e-scooters.

3
- **a** 70–74
- **b** 80–84
- **c** 0.2
- **d** About 1740
- **e** Can't tell for sure
  If one person survived until 100, it would not show up on the scale used.
- **f** In any order:
  People are living longer in 2021 than in 1952.
  The death rate for children, particularly babies, has decreased substantially since 1952.

Dot plots (pp. 47–50)

1
- **a** Summative
- **b** 13
- **c** 13
- **d** 0.1

2
- **a** 12
- **b** Restaurant B
  They had customers that gave them a 0 and a 10, whereas restaurant A scores were all between 1 and 9.
- **c** Either: Agree
  For restaurant B, 17 customers gave them 5 or more, but only 15 for restaurant A.
  Or: Can't tell for sure
  There is not a lot of difference between the two groups, so we would need more data to make the call.

3
- **a** Otago
- **b** 0.114 or $\frac{4}{35}$
- **c** 25.9%
- **d** Agree
  There are 227 beds in Hawkes Bay but only 189 in Otago.
- **e** Can't tell for sure
  We have no data on places to stay other than the standard DOC huts.

4 Right skew

5 Irregular

6 Bell shaped

7 Left skew

ISBN: 9780170451833

Scatter plots (pp. 51–55)

1 a

Day	Coordinates	Description
A	(**25**, **180**)	It was **25**°C and there were **180** visitors.
B	(**16**, **90**)	It was **16**°C and there were **90** visitors.
C	(**14**, **20**)	It was **14**°C and there were **20** visitors.

b It was only 16°C and yet there were 280 visitors.
c Agree
Mostly if it is cooler there are fewer people at the beach.
d i × This suggests that the decrease in visitors causes the temperature to drop.
ii ✓

2 a True b False
c True d False
e False
f Either: Agree
He spent a lot of time studying but got a very low grade.
Or: Can't tell for sure
He may have been feeling ill on the test day.
g Agree
He did very little study but he got one of the top grades.

3 **Direction:** negative.
Strength: moderate

4 **Direction:** positive
Strength: strong

5 **Direction:** positive
Strength: weak

6 **Direction:** negative
Strength: strong

7 The graph shows a **positive** relationship between a sugar consumption and the average number of decayed teeth. This means that people who consume more sugar tend to have **more** decayed teeth.

Statistical tables (pp. 56–59)

1 a 16
b 74%
c Can't tell for sure
There is only four years' worth of data. Drownings were low in 2020/2021, but it might be because it was a cold summer.

2 a 2.2 hours
b 6.6 hours
c 0.8 hour
d Agree
The mean time spent for the four age groups is 1.6 hours, and both 5–7 year olds and 8–11 year olds play on their own for longer than that.
e Agree
All the values in the bottom row of the table (Informal) are higher than those for Organised in the row above.

3 a 417 488
b 2021
c 992 372
d Either: Agree
Agree assuming every injury results in an ACC claim. The numbers of new and active claims have, overall, dropped over the six-year period.
Or: Can't tell for sure
This data is only for ACC claims. Not all injuries will result in a claim.
e Can't tell for sure
Medical costs increase with time, so it is more likely that equivalently serious injuries are becoming more expensive to treat.

4 a 29%
b 8.9
c 1 219 000
d Decreasing
e Disagree
Around 30% of homes have a dog, but only about 10% have fish.
f Agree
The percentage of households that have cats has decreased between 2011 and 2020, and so has the total number of cats.

Infographics (pp. 60–66)

1 a 89% from Total Readers list or 90% by adding areas in the infographic.
b 1%
c Fiction plus Non-fiction
d Agree
Only 29 or 30% read poetry.
e Agree
9% read only non-fiction, 1% read only poetry and 14% read only fiction, so just 24% read only one genre.

2 a They are removed in the waste water treatment facility.
b 17%
c 1 360 000
d 1 200 000
e 80 000

3 a 21% b 10%
c 4% d 36%

 ISBN: 9780170451833

4 **a** \$201 000 000 **b** 400 000
c \$110 **d** 24% per year
e Taranaki
f Agree
Wellington shoppers collectively spend \$658 million, whereas Waikato shoppers spend \$506 million.
g Can't tell for sure
The data is for eCommerce only, not people buying from actual shops. But Bay of Plenty eCommerce shoppers spend almost double the amount that those in Taranaki spend.

5 **a** 23.1%
b 22.7%
c 675 000
d ✓
✓
✗
✓

6 **a** 13 women **b** 6 adults
c $66.\dot{6}\%$
d $\frac{39}{80} \times 4\,000\,000 = 1\,950\,000$
e Agree
Only 14% of adults earn \$70 000 or more.
f Agree
More women (39%) than men (30%) earn less than \$70 001 per year and fewer women (5%) than men (9%) earn more than \$70 001 per year.

7 **a** 16, 17 or 18% **b** 20 000 or less
c Two vehicles
d Agree
As income increases, so does the line for households with three or more vehicles.
e Either: Disagree
The line for no vehicles does not appear to reach 0 at \$100 001 or more.
Or: Can't tell for sure
The scale on the map doesn't allow us to tell whether the line for no vehicles reaches 0 or not.

Data analysis (pp. 67–73)

Measures of centre (averages) (pp. 66–69)

1 Mean = 12.8 Median = 14
Mode = None
2 Mean = 1.76 Median = 1.45
Mode = 0.7 and 3.4
3 0, 2, 4, 4, 6, 6, 7, 9, 12, 13, 17, 19
Mean = 8.25 Median = 6.5
Mode = 4 and 6
4 Mean = 9.19 Median = 8.5
Mode = 8
5 Mean = 14.8 Median = 15
Mode = 15

Measure of spread (pp. 70–71)

1 Minimum = 5 LQ = 15 Median = 28.5
UQ = 41 Maximum = 53
Range = 48 Interquartile range = 26
2 Minimum = 12 LQ = 18 Median = 28
UQ = 34 Maximum = 40
Range = 28 Interquartile range = 16
3 Minimum = 2 LQ = 4.5 Median = 9
UQ = 15.5 Maximum = 20
Range = 18 Interquartile range = 11
4 Minimum = 11 LQ = 16.5 Median = 18
UQ = 18 Maximum = 20
Range = 9 Interquartile range = 1.5
5 Minimum = 11 LQ = 12.5 Median = 15
UQ = 18.5 Maximum = 20
Range = 9 Interquartile range = 6

Unusual features (pp. 72–73)

1 Median: 8.5 Mean: 11
The mean and the median are ~~similar~~/different.
The mean is larger because the data set is small so it is influenced by the 36 which is significantly bigger than the rest of the values.
2 Median: 18 Mean: $18.\dot{8}$
The mean and the median are similar/~~different.~~
They are similar because there are no extremely large or small values to influence the mean.
3 Median: 73 Mean: 63.6
The mean and the median are ~~similar~~/different.
The mean is smaller because the data set is small so it is influenced by the 2 which is significantly less than the rest of the values.
4 Median: 10.5 Mean: 10.3
The mean and the median are similar/~~different~~.
They are similar because, in the calculation of the mean, the smaller values of 6 and 7 are balanced by the 15 and 16.
5 Median: 15 Mean: 14.5 (1 dp)
The mean and the median are similar/~~different~~.
The 7 is much smaller than the rest of the data set, but it has little influence on the mean because the data set is larger than that in question **3**.

Box plots (pp. 74–79)

1

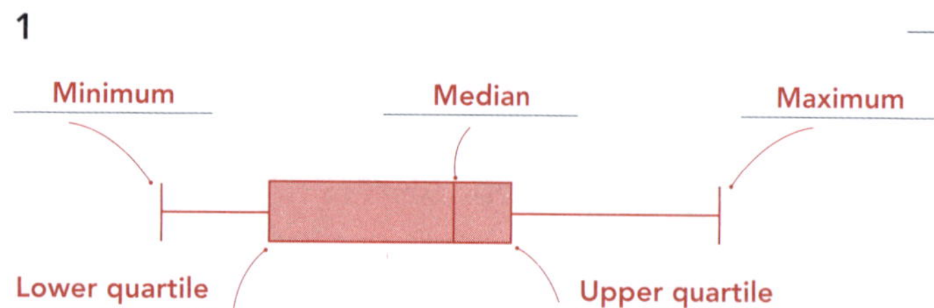

2

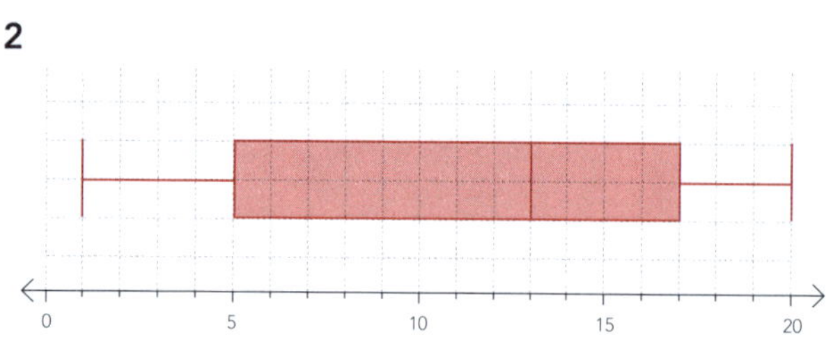

3 Minimum = 1 LQ = 7 Median = 12.5
UQ = 14.5 Maximum = 20

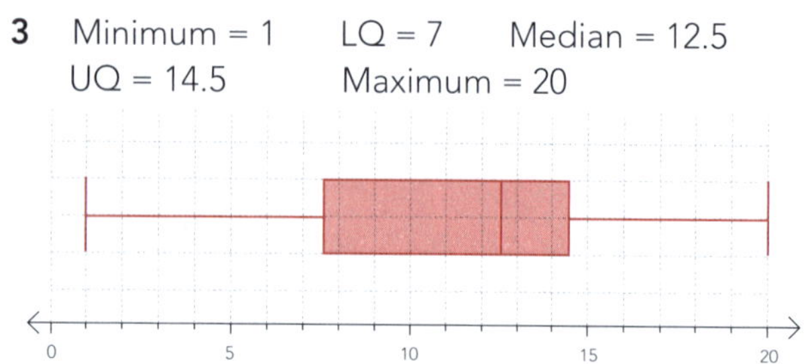

4 Minimum = 0 LQ = 3 Median = 6
UQ = 16 Maximum = 20

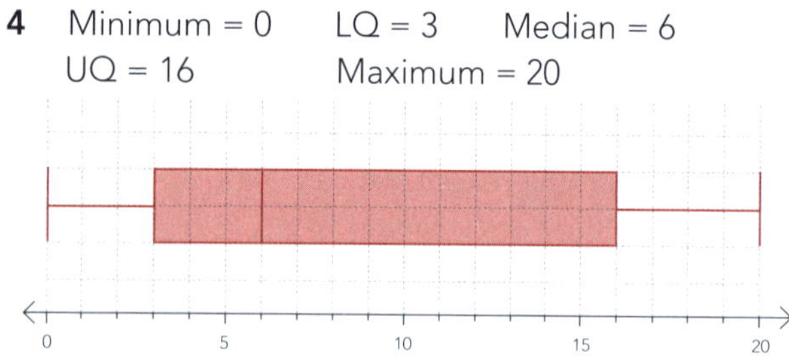

5 Minimum = 0.5 LQ = 4.5 Median = 6
UQ = 9.5 Maximum = 10

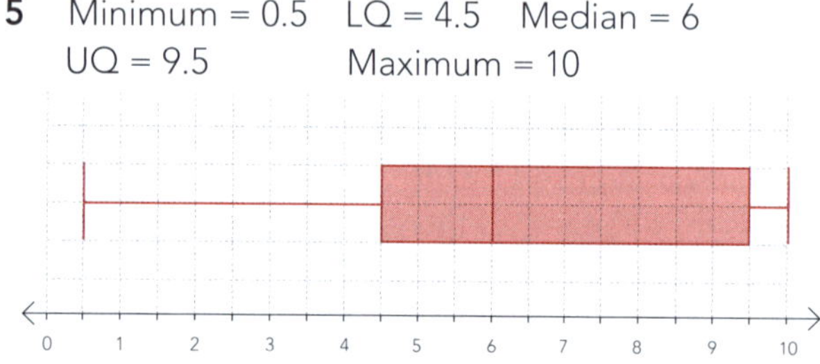

Understanding box plots (76–77)

1

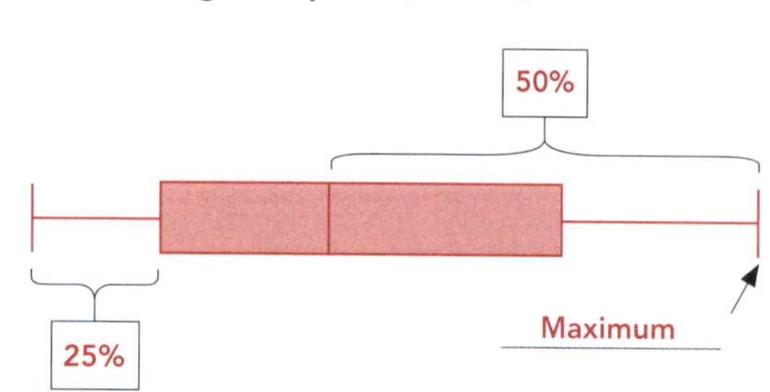

2

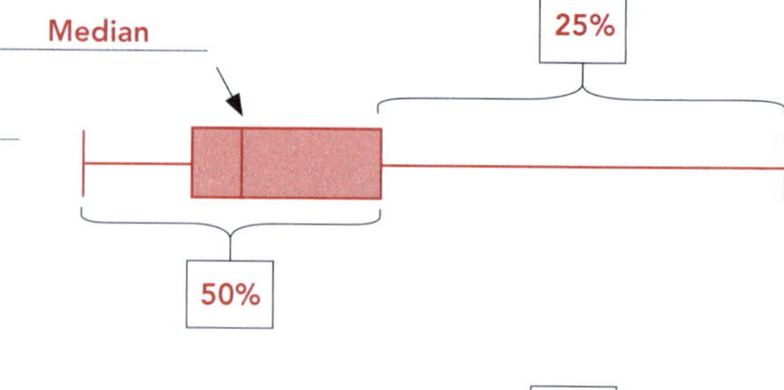

3

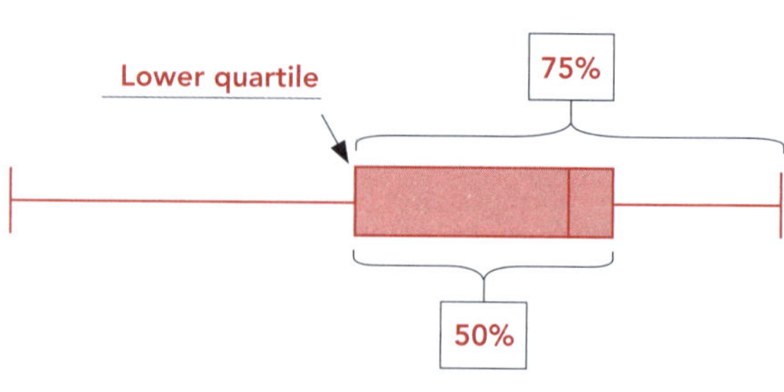

4

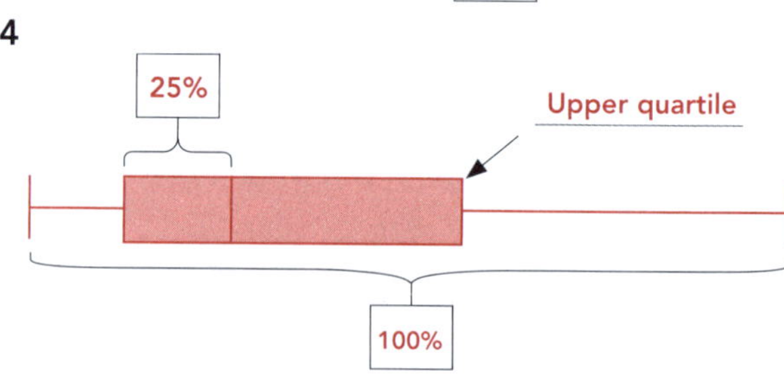

Comparing box plots (pp. 78–79)

1 a ✓ b ✓
c × d ✓

2 a ✓ b ✓
c ×

3 a Agree
Agree that this is true in general, because all the statistics on the Year 13 box plot are further to the right than those on the Year 9 plot.

b Either: Agree
Agree although there may be only one Year 9 student who is taller than 75% of Year 13 students.
Or: Can't tell for sure
There may be only one Year 9 student who is taller than 75% of Year 13 students.

4 a Either: Agree
Agree that this is true in general, because all the statistics on the box plot for right-handed students are further to the right than those on the left-handed plot.
Or: Can't tell for sure
There will be some left-handed students who are taller than right-handed students.

b Agree
The lengths of the whiskers on the right end of the box plots are not very long.

ISBN: 9780170451833

Challenge 2 (p. 80)

1 A
2 C
3 B
4 A dot plot shows the values of each piece of data.
5 The values of the median and quartiles.
6 Both give a picture of the distribution of the data.

Challenge 3 (p. 81)

1 a ✓ b maybe
c maybe d ×
2 a 3 b 4
c 2 d 1

3

	Similar	Different
a		✓
b	✓	
c	✓	

Revision 1 (pp. 82–84)

1 $\frac{2}{9} = 0.\dot{2}$ $\frac{7}{35} = 0.2$ More likely: $\frac{2}{9}$

2 'How tall are you?' is an example of a **summary** question, and the answer will produce **continuous** data.

3 a

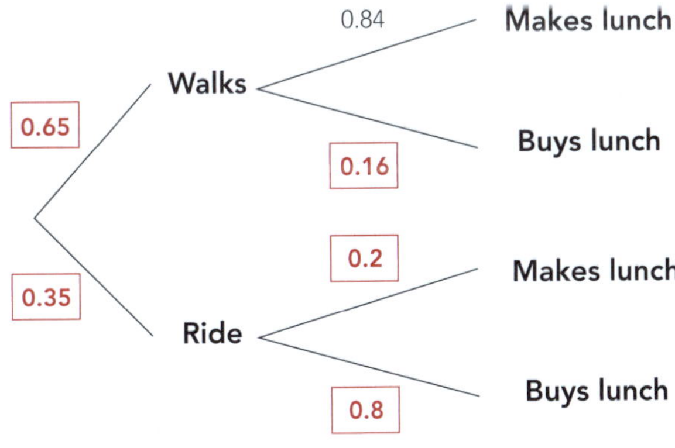

b 0.28
c 0.616

4 take a sample

5 a discrete
b Eye colour, hair colour, favourite chocolate, favourite movie, etc.
(If your answer is different, check with your teacher.)
c continuous

6 descriptive

7 a 25–29 year olds
b 5
c 75–79 years old
d Agree
In almost every age category, more males than females have their vehicles stolen.
e Either: Agree
There are far fewer thefts of vehicles belonging to over 50 year olds.
Or: Can't tell for sure
The thieves probably don't know that a vehicle belongs to an old person. It just might be that older people drive vehicles less attractive to thieves, or they take more precautions to make stealing the vehicle difficult.

8 a ✓
b ×
c ✓

9 a Asian
b 20.6%
c 0.056 (2 sf)

Revision 2 (pp. 85–87)

1 36 in 95 = 0.379 $\frac{19}{50} = 0.38$ More likely: $\frac{19}{50}$

2 'How many Year 13 boys and how many Year 13 girls have driver licences?' is an example of a **comparative** question, and the answer will produce **descriptive** data.

3 a

	Food technology	Digital technology	Mechanics	Totals
Year 9	62	36	45	143
Year 10	57	39	29	125
Totals	119	75	74	268

b $\frac{119}{268} = 0.44$ (2 dp)
c 0.534
d $\frac{45}{268} = 0.17$ (2 dp)
e 31.2%

4 do a census

5 a descriptive
b Shoe size, number of anything. (If your answer is different, check with your teacher.)
c descriptive

6 Discrete and descriptive data

7 'Did you have a bath this morning?' is an example of ~~an open~~/a closed question.

8 a Cooper
b Hugo

ISBN: 9780170451833

c 10

d Between 2014 and 2015 and between 2019 and 2020.

e Can't tell for sure
While it's the most popular of the three names in 2021, it doesn't mean it will be in 2022.

f Agree
In fact, more than twice the number of babies were named Braxton as Hugo.

9 a True b False
c True d True

10 a 45–54 years
b Can't tell for sure
This would depend on the definition of old!

 ISBN: 9780170451833